PRACTICAL
PRODUCTIVITY

PRACTICAL PRODUCTIVITY

A Guide to Surviving
Life's Juggling Act

MONISHA KUMAR LONGACRE

Published by Ripples Media
www.ripples.media

Copyright © 2025 by Monisha Longacre

All rights reserved. No part of this book may be reproduced or used in any manner without written permission of the copyright owner except for the use of quotations in a book review. For more information: publishing@ripples.media

First printing 2025

Cover design & book interior by Carolyn Asman

ISBN 979-8-9926212-0-4 Paperback
ISBN 979-8-9926212-1-1 Hardback
ISBN 979-8-9926212-2-8 E-book

For My Daddy
who inspired me
to be good,
do good,
and spread goodness
every single day.

TABLE OF CONTENTS

FOREWORD 13

INTRODUCTION 17

YOUR TIME 21
    The Myth of Time Management 25
    The Time Paradox 28
    Making the Most of Your Time 32
    It's All About Time Blocking 35
    Double or Nothing 38
    The Constraints of Procrastination 41
    To Multitask or Not to Multitask? 44
    Sleep is Not Wasted Time 47

YOUR LISTS 51
    Your Life in Lists 55
    The Magic of A Single To-Do List 58
    The Perfect To-Do List is a Prioritized One ... 61
    The Most Important Tasks 64
    The Lingering Task 67
    The "To-Don't" List 70
    The "Done" List 72
    The "Someday" List 75
    Enjoy Happier Holidays with Lists 79
    Cultivating Your Lists 82

YOUR STUFF 85
    A Place for Everything 89
    Less is More 92

The Three-Bin System 96
The Shopping List.. 99
Achieve Balance By Maximizing Your Tools.. 102
I Forgot My Phone... And I Survived 106
Productive Packing for Your Next Trip 110

YOUR DAY 113
Start Each Day By Making Your Bed................ 117
A Perfectly Productive Day 120
Eat That Frog.. 124
Go With the Flow 127
The Power of a Shower 130
The Two-Minute Rule 133
So Many Inboxes, So Much Wasted Time 136
Arrive on Time Every Time.................................. 140
Making Meetings Work Again 143
The Fallacy of Doing It All................................... 146

YOUR LIFE 149
One Balanced Life to Live.................................... 153
Make Smarter Resolutions.................................. 156
Bringing Your Vision to Life................................ 159
The Prioritization Puzzle...................................... 162
The Juggling Act... 166
Big Rocks and Little Rocks.................................. 170
The Three List Assessment................................. 173
The Rule of Three... 176
Getting Over Feeling Overwhelmed 178
Managing Your Energy 181
Always Have a Plan "B".. 184
The Value of Being Organized 187

YOUR EFFECTIVENESS 191
Productivity Requires Perseverance................ 195
The Importance of Why 198
Five Productivity Pitfalls....................................... 201
The Biggest Productivity Problem..................... 204
The Three R's of Productivity.............................. 207
How Being Busy Breeds Productivity............... 210
Don't Break the Chain 213
Creating New Habits.. 217
The Productivity Workout 220
Just Say No!.. 223
Asking for Help is Not a Weakness 226
Feedback is a Gift 229

UNTIL NEXT TIME... 233

APPENDIX.. 235

PRIORIGAMI 239

REFERENCES 241

RESOURCES 245

ACKNOWLEDGMENTS 247

ABOUT THE AUTHOR 249

FOREWORD

Early in my career, I attended a leadership conference. I followed the crowd that first morning into the large lecture hall and found myself listening to a fireside chat with the leader of one of the largest technology companies in the world. About halfway through the interview, when asked how he manages his schedule, his response changed how I have viewed time management ever since:

"I used to believe that my bursting-at-the-seams calendar directly embodied how effective I was as a leader."

I nodded my head along with most of the audience because that's exactly how I saw my calendar.

"It wasn't until a few years back," he continued, "that I realized just how incredibly wrong that viewpoint is. First, a full calendar means you have no time to think. At best, you're just reacting as you bounce from meeting to meeting, ending each day exhausted. But more importantly, as a leader, you must be able to help where and when needed. This is why I now view my calendar completely opposite of how I used to. The more open spaces, the more I'll be able to think strategically about my goals and the more flexible I can be with my time throughout the week."

As shocking and impactful as his main point was, I was most struck by how strategic he was about managing his time. It was obvious that his success could be tied directly to his ability to manage his time effectively.

Since then, I've tried hard to manage my time and energy strategically. Like Monisha, I've tried every to-do system imaginable, read every book on prioritization available, and implemented every efficiency philosophy I could get my hands on.

Over the last twenty years, I felt like I'd become somewhat of an expert on "getting stuff done."

That is until I met Monisha.

It's one thing to try every time management app; it's an entirely different thing to create your own. Likewise, most people are content with *reading* time management books. Monisha, seeing a better way, decided to *write* one.

Monisha has such a distinctive view on this topic, and she lays it out organized and logically. (Imagine that!) She talks about concepts we all know and love, like to-do lists and calendar management, while also adding in things that caught me by surprise, such as keeping an entertainment list and the importance of sleep!

Perhaps my favorite topic in this book is the often overlooked but pesky 'lingering tasks.' You know, those tasks you've had on your list forever, and you can't quite figure out what to do with them. Well, this book will give you the answer.

And while this book is mainly geared toward adults, I think it's equally important for the younger generation (perhaps the focus of a future edition?). Every time I get a chance to impart wisdom to a young person, I implore them to learn how to manage their time effectively. (Maybe one day, this kind of executive skill will be taught in high school or college.)

What you prioritize and how you manage your time directly correlates to how successful you will be and, perhaps more importantly, how happy you will be.

That's why the book you have in your hands is so important. Critical, even. The more people are able to accomplish their goals, the better the world will be. I'm excited to put many of Monisha's principles into action, and I know after reading this book, you will be, too.

Jeff Hilimire
Serial entrepreneur and author of
The Turnaround Leadership Series

INTRODUCTION

Some time ago, I was a vice president managing weather.com at The Weather Channel, which was a top fifteen consumer website at the time. I had two very active young children. My husband was a partner at Ernst & Young, traveling weekly to one client or another. While we were living in Atlanta, my extended family still lived where I grew up in Northern Virginia, so I didn't have much local support.

While I had a full and very fulfilling life, I didn't sleep much, didn't work out, and didn't eat very well, but I was happy. After all, I was doing all the things I had dreamed of in terms of achieving the goal of "having it all." I was checking off all the "necessary" boxes – family, education, friends, career, marriage, cars, children, house, vacations, beach condo, and so on.

One day, over lunch a colleague of mine looked directly at me and thoughtfully asked, "How do you do it all?" Well, that was a very interesting question. I honestly hadn't given it much thought. My immediate reaction was, "I don't know. I just do it."

A few days later, I thought about this question again. I realized that there were some things that were innate. For example, I am never late, I don't procrastinate, I make my bed every day, and I can't remember a time when I didn't have a to-do list. On the other hand, I had to learn other techniques through trial and error. And, as my life became more demanding and complicated, I certainly had to train myself and practice how to juggle and prioritize tasks, how to stay focused, when and how to say, "no," and how to accept that it is OK to let a ball drop every now and then.

As I spent more time thinking through how I approached my days, I started to realize that over the years, I had cobbled together various systems and processes that enabled me to manage my life. I grew more conscious of how I was prioritizing my tasks and focusing my time and energy. I also became more aware of the things that were wasting my time and tried to find smarter ways to tackle them. For me, it was a game – identify a problem or opportunity, and then find a better way to do it.

In my quest to figure out how to optimize my life, I picked up all of the productivity books I could get my hands on (see the Reference section for a list). I voraciously read them and tested the various recommendations, tactics, processes, and techniques to determine what worked best.

I would try several different systems to find the ones that were the most effective and useful. Not everything I tried worked. I also found that not all of them stuck. Some were effective for a while and then I would just stop utilizing them for one reason or another. I also realized that some took a little while to become habit-forming. Others worked like magic. More than a few, I am still working on.

Over the years, I thought about capturing these practices in some form or another to help others who were also trying to do it all. For several years, I published an online blog, hoping that some of these insights might inspire others to try some of my practical productivity hacks. I even created my own task management app called priorigami. I also imagined writing a book and sharing all of my learned best practices so others could also benefit from my knowledge, experimentation, and real-life experiences.

And, here it is – finally! It could have happened sooner if I had taken my own advice. And, to be perfectly honest, I was able to find the time and the focus to write this book, while working two different COO jobs and relaunching my productivity app, by following the recommendations outlined in this book.

This book is full of short, practical productivity tips and tricks to help you actually do everything you want to do simply by changing your approach. While there are countless tools and technologies that can help you, this book is primarily about examining your mindset. It's about helping you find the right framework to solve the productivity puzzle and make life easier for you and those around you.

This book is presented as a helpful how-to guide, rather than a fictional novel. While you can read it from start to finish, it doesn't necessarily have to be read cover to cover. It is written so that you can read a chapter or two on a relevant topic of interest and pick up a handful of ideas or tips you can try. My hope is that reading this book for even 15 to 20 minutes could save hours of your time. Or, as we say when pitching a new project at work, reading *Practical Productivity* was designed to have a very high ROI!

Since many of the recommendations are related to or build upon one another, I've included a READ MORE section at the end of every chapter which cross references other relevant chapters in the book. These suggestions allow you to further explore the topic and bounce around the book which might work better than simply reading it sequentially. The goal is to find what works best for you.

Keep in mind that not all of these tactics will work for you. Some won't make any sense. Some may need to be tweaked or adjusted, and others you may adopt instantly and wonder why you hadn't made the change sooner. Just consider trying those that resonate the most and see what happens – it could be magical.

I hope you'll keep this book on hand and these tactics in mind for the next time you find yourself struggling or feeling overwhelmed. You might find a tip or two to help you survive life's juggling act and thrive as you make the most of every moment.

YOUR TIME

---

*Time is more valuable than money.
You can get more money,
but you cannot get more time.*

Jim Rohn

YOUR TIME

Time is at the heart of everything we do.

There's not enough time. I am running out of time. Now's the time. Time to go. Time's up. All in good time. We had the time of our lives. Time and time again. Only time will tell. In due time. It's a race against time. We're just killing time. Time is money. Good times. Bad times. We're having a whale of a time. Story time. Party time. Closing time. Quitting time. If only we could turn back time. Time stood still. Time after time. In the nick of time. Time is on my side. Times like these. Too much time on my hands. One more time. One last time. Once in a lifetime. (By the way, how many songs came rushing back to you while reading this list? Check out my "All About Time" playlist by monishaklongacre on Spotify!)

Whether we acknowledge it or not, time is our most valuable asset and most prized possession. We measure it carefully from nanoseconds to eras and eons and everything in between. We celebrate timely milestones, from birth to death, from start to finish, and from first date to every anniversary thereafter.

We wear smartwatches, look at the clock, and ask each other what time it is multiple times a day – all in an ongoing, never-ending effort to manage our time.

But, how do we make sure we're making the best use of the time we have? How are we maximizing every moment? How can we optimize the time we're given? The clock is ticking away… every second, every minute, every hour of every day.

In the next few chapters, we'll think about why managing "time" is virtually impossible and how it's so challenging given the finite number of hours in each day. I'll share some thoughts about how to look at managing your time slightly differently, as well as outline some ideas about time blocking, procrastinating, multitasking, and even sleeping.

Never forget that time is fleeting. And so, this is the perfect place to begin our discussion on improving our productivity. Let's get right to it.

After all, we don't have any time to waste.

1

THE MYTH OF TIME MANAGEMENT

So many of us talk about time management. Countless articles have been written and tools have been created to help us manage our time. There are time management gurus, tutorials, and classes. Half of our working day is spent juggling our calendars in a never-ending attempt to "manage our time."

But, what if we cannot control time? Would managing our time be a completely useless exercise? If you think about it, no matter what we do, time continues to tick forward. We cannot rewind it and we cannot fast forward it. It just is and it continues according to its plan – each second, every minute, the next hour and then into the next day.

When you really think about it, it becomes clear that, in fact, we simply cannot control time. Instead we should rethink what we're trying to "manage" and reorient our focus to the things that we can and do control: our priorities, our energy, and our attention.

PRIORITIES

Each day we all have more to do than we can handle. We know what needs to get done and we constantly make choices about what's most important and what needs to be prioritized. Setting clear and deliberate priorities is the single-most critical factor driving our productivity and future success. We control how we spend our time even if we cannot control time itself.

ENERGY

We also decide how to spend our energy. Energy is finite and to optimize output, it's imperative that we focus our efforts and our energy on the most important priorities. These days, this is harder to do than it seems due to the countless distractions that get in our way. So often, we expend more of our energy on the things that are seemingly urgent but not all that important.

ATTENTION

Focus seems to be a lost art, especially for me. With countless dings, pings, alerts, and notifications, it's virtually impossible to focus on any one thing for an extended period. Personally, I struggle with this constantly. Research has shown that multitasking is not possible and simply does not work. (We'll get deeper into this as well.)

To be most productive it behooves us to focus our full attention on one task at a time. After trying various methods, I found that the Pomodoro technique works best for me. Named after a "pomodoro," or tomato kitchen timer, this time management method suggests breaking down your work into set intervals followed by scheduled breaks. To reduce interruptions and improve focus, set a timer for 25 minutes to work on a set task and then take a 5 to 10 minute break between intervals.

Instead of using a pomodoro kitchen timer, I set a timer on my phone for 20 minutes of focused time and then reward myself with a 10-minute break at the end to check notifications, emails, and socials. At first, it was really hard for me to do this. I would set the timer and every few minutes would check how much time had passed.

It didn't pass very quickly. During my focused time, I would still reach for my phone or check my email. But in time, I got used to it and now I find that 20 minutes flies by quite quickly.

Experiment with this technique to find the right length of time that allows you to focus and do your best work uninterrupted.

> **TRY THIS**
>
> Do you spend a lot of time trying to manage your time? Does it actually work for you? Instead, think about how you could start better managing your priorities, energy, and attention. Spend a day or two focusing on one of these three areas. Do you find that you can manage it better?

> **READ MORE**
>
> The Prioritization Puzzle
> Managing Your Energy
> Five Productivity Pitfalls

2

THE TIME PARADOX

We've all heard it and said it ourselves many times: "There just aren't enough hours in the day to get it all done." And, through my analysis, I found that this is indeed the case. Not having enough time is not just a feeling, but an actual reality that we all face every day.

In my research on productivity, I consistently find that the most productive people don't just work hard but they take care of themselves as well. So, I decided to experiment with my time each day to try to find the optimal use of every hour, but the reality is that there simply are not enough hours in the day.

It's a very simple math problem. Let's start by looking at the two "big rocks" which basically account for two thirds of your day right off the bat.

- 8 hours for a good night's sleep
- 8 hours at work (at least)

Next, let's add in the minimum necessary things that we must do every day:

- 1 1/2 hours to prepare and eat three meals
- 1 hour to get ready
- 1 hour to commute
- 30 minutes for household chores

That leaves us with less than 4 hours to take care of everything else that we should be doing to be healthy and productive, including:

- 1 hour to exercise
- 1 hour to spend with family
- 1 hour to read
- 30 minutes for mindfulness (meditation, yoga, or journaling, etc.)

But now, there's no time left for the following fun activities on which we would rather – and often do – spend our time doing, including:

- Watching TV
- Socializing
- Checking social media
- Entertaining
- Shopping
- Playing games or sports

To make time for the things we like to do, we often neglect the things we should be doing. We skimp on the amount of sleep we get, avoid taking mental breaks, and limit exercising to just a few times a week simply because there are not enough hours in the day.

Here's a visual breakdown of how one could ideally spend their time compared to how many of us actually end up spending our time:

HOURS SPENT EACH DAY

	Ideal	Actual
Sleeping	8	7
Working	8	9
Commuting	1	1
Eating	1.5	1
Getting Ready	1	1
Housework	1	1
Exercising	1	0
Reading	1	0
Family Time	1	1
Mindfulness	0.5	0
Watching TV	0	2
Online Activities	0	1
	24	24

One of my favorite TV shows was 24 which featured Jack Bauer, (played by Kiefer Sutherland) a federal agent in the US Counter-Terrorism Unit (CTU). Each season covered a 24-hour period where they'd have to save the United States from different security threats. Interestingly, each episode depicted one hour in real-time with a bold countdown clock ticking down the remaining seconds and resulted in an intense heart-pounding, high-stress experience. And they capitalized on every single second of the day because they didn't sleep, eat, rest, socialize, or even go to the bathroom! How's that for making the most of every second of the day?

TRY THIS

For the next few days track how you spend each hour of your day. How does it compare to the ideal breakdown of time? What are you spending more time on than you should and what are you not doing that you need to find time to do? Are there ways to adjust your schedule to find that optimal balance?

READ MORE

A Perfectly Productive Day
Big Rocks and Little Rocks

3

MAKING THE MOST OF YOUR TIME

How often do we say or hear the sentiment: "I'm super busy and I just don't have enough time?" When asked how we are doing, we often just instantly and thoughtlessly respond: "I'm so busy."

Sometimes, being busy, overbooked, and frazzled is seen as a sign of success. Perhaps it shows that we are wanted and needed. It could be that it makes us feel important. Or, maybe it's our way of projecting our productivity. But being busy and being productive are not necessarily one in the same.

Time is one of our greatest treasures and how we use our time is critical to improving productivity. Are you spending your time on the most important things? Do you find time slipping away without getting anything done? Are you running around all day but not accomplishing anything meaningful?

To make the most of your time, make sure you focus on the most important things first and foremost, and when you are most energetic and productive.

So, what's most important? When considering taking on or starting a new task, think about these questions to determine if it's a good use of your time:

- How does doing this task benefit you?
- Does it align with your current goals?

- Are there any dependencies or deadlines?
- Can it be done later?
- Could someone else do it?
- What is the impact of deciding not to do it?
- If you do it, what won't get done?

Based on your answers to these questions, pick your top three tasks for the day and then plan *when* you'll get them done. Selecting your priorities is just the start. By scheduling the task, you'll be blocking time to actually focus on completing the task. This will also force you to plan what is specifically involved in getting it done so you can evaluate how much time it'll take to complete. By going through this process, you will also begin to visualize yourself doing and completing the task which can be very motivating.

Keep in mind that it's not about not having enough time, it's just a matter of how you decide to spend your time.

TRY THIS

Review your calendar for last week to assess which things were a waste of your time and figure out how to eliminate them going forward. Then, look to the week ahead and plan how you're going to spend your time on the tasks and appointments that really matter. Start to consider the best times to tackle tasks when your focus and energy levels are at their highest. We'll examine this practice further later on.

READ MORE

The Most Important Tasks
A Perfectly Productive Day
The Importance of Why
How Being Busy Breeds Productivity

4

IT'S ALL ABOUT TIME BLOCKING

Being productive starts with good time management. Most of us use some sort of calendar to manage our time. We are good about jotting down appointments, scheduling meetings, and noting deadlines. But, what happens in between those scheduled time slots is our biggest missed opportunity.

For years, I have used a methodology popularized by Cal Newport in his book, *Deep Work*, called "time blocking" or, as I fondly refer to it, my version of "productivity Tetris."[1] Here's how you play.

At the beginning of every week pick a set time to start the game. First, review your calendar for the week ahead to make sure all of your appointments and meetings have been entered and are up-to-date. Next, make note of the things you must get done that week and start slotting them into the open spaces on your calendar, making sure you schedule them ahead of any deadlines. At the beginning or end of each day, review and confirm your schedule, and then pick the top three things you need to get done and slot them in between your scheduled items.

Be sure to block times to handle recurring tasks such as submitting your timesheet at the end of the week or your expense report at the end of the month, paying your bills weekly, taking a daily walk, or doing yoga several times a week. By blocking these time slots you'll have set aside the necessary time to make sure these things get done on time and you'll avoid forgetting about them or rushing to get them done at the last minute.

Once your day is fully time blocked you simply work through it according to the plan. Always allow for more time to complete a task than you think is necessary. If you finish the task sooner than the allotted time you can always reward yourself with a break – a snack, a podcast or video, or a quick chat with a friend.

If, and when, something comes up that disrupts your day, then it's time to play "Tetris" and rearrange your time blocks. First, determine how to make time for the disruption and then reshuffle the other time blocks. By doing this, you're sure to have dedicated time for the things you want to get done.

If your calendar supports it, try color coding your time blocks so you can visually see how you're spending your time and to make it easier to identify which blocks can be moved around.

Time blocking also works to set reminders for certain tasks that need to be done on a certain date or by a certain time in the future. For instance, I schedule time to pay my bills. I also schedule reminders for when reservations can be made or tickets go on sale. You can also block time to cancel or renew subscriptions. I even block time when the next season of my favorite show is going to be released.

TRY THIS

Find time to look at the week ahead. Are all of your meetings and appointments on your calendar? Think about how you are spending your time. What other things do you need to get done? Be sure to block times to complete those tasks. Don't forget to schedule time for the things you want to do as well.

READ MORE

Double or Nothing
A Perfectly Productive Day

5

DOUBLE OR NOTHING

I was trying to schedule a meeting with a very busy working mother who was reluctant to commit to a meeting time. After digging in further, I found out that work often required her attention to last-minute requests with quick turnarounds and as a result, she didn't feel like she had control of her schedule. She shared that she often avoids scheduling meetings or appointments for fear of letting someone down by needing to cancel at the last minute. This reluctance extended into her social life as well.

More often than not life gets in the way of our plans and impacts our schedules. While it's critical to plan and schedule your time to maximize productivity, the reality is that things change and calendars have to be adjusted. In fact, sometimes we need to plan for a change in plans.

One handy trick that I've used for years and has saved me many times is to "double book." It's simple. If something needs to get done, schedule it into your day. And, if it's really important, schedule it again at a later time. Yes, go ahead and book two times to ensure that if something comes up and disrupts the first window, you already have a backup plan in place.

This works for exercising as well. If you really want to make sure that you get to the gym or go for a run, schedule time to do it. And then, find a second time to make sure that if something prevents you from doing it at the first scheduled time, you still have time to get it done in the backup window.

It's a bit more challenging but you can do this for critical and time-sensitive meetings as well. First, set expectations with the meeting participant that your schedule often gets disrupted with urgent, last-minute requests but that meeting with them is really important to you so you would like to book two meeting times in case the first one falls through. Nobody has ever turned this down or questioned it. In fact, most are pretty open to it and think it's a pretty smart idea.

I have also done this to make sure I meet a friend for dinner. Pick a date that works and then find and block a second date as a backup.

And, as an added bonus, when you get your task completed or meeting done during the first scheduled spot, your second one opens up some valuable time on your calendar to do something else or have some fun. It's always nice to delete an appointment and see some unexpected time open up in my day. It's like finding money in a jacket pocket!

TRY THIS

Pick something that you really need to get done this week. Schedule time for it and then schedule a second block of time later in the week to make sure it gets done. You win either by having a backup plan in place, or by opening up extra time on your calendar.

READ MORE

It's All About Time Blocking
The Most Important Things

6

THE CONSTRAINTS OF PROCRASTINATION

Do you wait until the last minute to get something done? Do you need an immediate and impending deadline looming over you to get motivated or to focus? I personally have never been a procrastinator. I am the annoying person that plans how to get things done as soon as I'm given the assignment or the thought arises.

But some people have a disposition to procrastinate through no fault of their own. Procrastinators simply don't get the same dopamine hit from getting things done. And, if there's no apparent upside for doing something, why rush to do it?

At some point, all of us have put off doing something that's unpleasant or challenging or just plain boring. We tend to prioritize doing the things we enjoy and those with the biggest immediate rewards. Unfortunately, those things aren't always the most important or the ones with long-term impact.

While there's nothing wrong with procrastinating – so long as the work gets done by the deadline – here are some limiting factors that could impact those who wait until the last minute.

NO TIME TO REVIEW OR REVISE

If you're working on a paper or proposal right up against the deadline, you won't have time to set the work aside and review it from a fresh frame of mind. Taking time away from a deliverable and coming back to it after some time can give you a new perspective and you will notice grammatical errors or typos or angles that you may have missed.

NO TIME FOR EMERGENCIES

I always chuckle when I hear the adage "burning the midnight oil." I picture someone handwriting a paper with an ink pen late into the night next to an oil lamp. I assume they had a deadline and waited until the last minute and the power was out, their laptop battery was dead, and that's their last resort. If you procrastinate, your ability to deal with unforeseen emergencies is severely limited. As some may say, you leave yourself with no breathing room.

NO TIME FOR OTHER OPTIONS

For me, the biggest reason I don't like to procrastinate is because I want to be open to opportunities that may come my way. I want to be able to accept last-minute dinner invitations or to use someone's tickets to a concert or sporting event that they can no longer attend. I love to get an unexpected call from a long-lost friend and have the time to catch up for an hour. Or, how about an impromptu get together with a few friends?

If you're working on something up until the deadline, you end up having to decline these opportunities.

TRY THIS

Is there something you've been putting off? Why are you procrastinating? Is there a way for you to break the project down into smaller pieces that might not be so overwhelming and easier for you to tackle? Are any of the constraints listed above enough to motivate you not to wait until the last minute?

READ MORE

Making the Most of Your Time
The Lingering Task
The Prioritization Puzzle

7

TO MULTITASK OR NOT TO MULTITASK?

We all do it. I certainly do. Even though we all know that multitasking doesn't work very well. But, in the constant quest to save time, why not knock two things out at once? Kill two birds with one stone? Sounds like a smart plan. But does it actually help you save time?

Science says convincingly that multitasking is not an efficient use of time. In fact, in his book, *Hyperfocus: How to Manage Your Attention in a World of Distraction*, Chris Bailey shared, "When we continually switch between tasks, our work takes 50 percent longer, compared with doing one task from start to completion."[2]

Our brains simply cannot focus on doing two things at once. When we do things simultaneously, our brain is constantly switching back and forth between managing the two tasks. The process of task or context switching ends up depleting our energy and ability to focus. Not to mention that it also negatively impacts the quality of our work. Sounds exhausting, doesn't it?

Even though I know this fact, for some reason I'm very stubborn on this point. I keep thinking I can handle two things at once. While "watching TV" I reply to text messages, and I inevitably end up having to rewatch key parts of the show I've missed. This is hardly a good use of my time or very relaxing.

Nowadays, when I'm watching a show or movie I really want to focus on and enjoy, I try to put my devices in the other room so I'm not tempted to do a quick check. And, if I impulsively reach to pick up my phone or laptop while watching a show, I make myself stop and choose one. I force myself to decide whether to pick up my phone and pause the show or continue to watch and wait to get on my devices.

During an online video or webinar, I often find myself checking emails and after reading and responding to a few of them, the webinar content is lost on me. I may be one of the few, but I can't even pay attention to a podcast or audiobook while walking. My mind wanders as I take in everything around me and I have no clue what I just heard. So instead of getting two things done, in effect, I have wasted my time and inevitably have to go back and rewatch or re-listen to what I've missed.

But all is not completely lost. I can do two things at once so long as one is somewhat routine and mindless or if I am using two very different parts of my brain. I am pretty good at folding laundry and watching TV. I am also good at driving and listening to music. I excel at thinking while taking a shower. While I cannot listen to a book while walking, I am very good at talking to a friend.

But I am most proud of my ability to read and type at the same time, thanks to the typing class elective I took in high school. But it took a lot of practice to train my brain to learn how to do this. And, by far the one multitasking activity I love the most – I can enjoy a glass of red wine while reading a book!

TRY THIS

What happens when you try to multitask? Is it effective or do you find that one task suffers? Next time try to do one thing at a time. Do you find it's easier to focus and is the quality of your work better? On the flip side, which two things can you successfully do at the same time?

READ MORE

The Fallacy of Doing It All
The Juggling Act
Creating New Habits

SLEEP IS NOT WASTED TIME

When I was a teenager, I loved my sleep. I would regularly sleep until noon and sometimes later (to my parents' chagrin). They simply couldn't understand how I could sleep that much. Neither did I. But I enjoyed it.

Once I got to college my sleeping habits flipped to the other extreme. I hardly slept at all, and it wasn't because I was studying or partying all night. I worked full-time at the student-run daily newspaper on top of a full load of classes and yes, I still wanted to have a full college experience as well.

My job as Operations Manager was to "roll the paper" and send it off to the printer nightly Sunday through Thursday. Our goal was to be done by 11 p.m. but that rarely happened. On big news days, we would be heading home as the sun rose. During those days it was normal for me to get an average of four to five hours of sleep a night.

This was a great trial run for when I was a full-time working mother with two young kids. Sleep became a "nice to have" and quite honestly, I can't remember nights I would sleep more than six hours or so. Thankfully I was still relatively young so somehow, I managed to keep up.

At a later point, when my kids started sleeping in more and our schedules weren't as hectic with early-morning commitments, I was able to get more rest. When I extended my sleep schedule to a daily average of seven to eight hours, I finally began to realize the real benefits of sleep, including physical relief as my eyes no longer burned during my morning shower. I admit I had begun to accept that burning as normal. Apparently when you don't get enough sleep, your eyes don't produce enough tears which can make your eyes dry and itchy. Who knew?

If you're having trouble falling asleep, consider changing your bedtime routine. Do you watch TV or scroll through social media before bedtime? Try stopping at least 30 minutes before going to bed and instead pick up a book, take a hot shower, or listen to calming music. If you find your mind racing when your head hits the pillow, spend a few minutes making a list or writing in a journal to get those thoughts out of your head.

If you wake up in the middle of the night and have trouble falling asleep, find a mental exercise or practice to help you get back to sleep quickly. One piece of advice that works really well for me is to not look at the time when I wake up. I have turned my alarm clock around so I can't see the time. This prevents me from worrying about how much sleep I've gotten or how soon I have to get up.

I also use the military sleep method to help me get back to sleep quickly. It takes some practice so give yourself time to get used to it before you give it up. The basic principle is to relax your whole body, focus on your breathing, and repeat the mantra, "Don't think."

Here are some additional reasons why getting enough sleep is a good investment of your time.

BETTER HEALTH

While you sleep, your body gets to work repairing, restoring, and recharging. These activities result in better physical and mental health, reduced risk of serious health problems, and improved memory and mood. Sounds like a miracle drug, doesn't it? It also doesn't cost anything and doesn't have any negative side effects!

BETTER OUTPUT

When you are well-rested, your productivity will improve. Your ideas are more creative, your throughput increases, and the quality of your work improves as well. A rested brain and body can function at its optimal level and instead of trudging through each day, you can seamlessly and effortlessly sail through the day.

BETTER RELATIONSHIPS

When you sleep well, you aren't as irritable and testy as when you're tired. Too many times, I unnecessarily snapped at someone who didn't deserve it, and I immediately apologized by saying, "I'm really sorry. It's not you, I'm just really tired."

Honestly, that's not a very good excuse. After a good night of sleep, you're naturally calmer and happier and those around you can tell the difference and appreciate your good mood much more.

Bonus Tip: For years, I would set my alarm and leap out of bed as soon as it went off. I was not a snoozer. I just thought when you wake up, you automatically get up. I was wrong about that as well. (Thankfully my fellow Mom friends clued me into this fact!) When you can, spend some time in bed after waking up. Use this time to stretch or breathe or visualize the day ahead. Taking some time for yourself before you dive into the hectic pace of the day pays dividends later.

Reality Check: While there are many benefits to sleep, I recognize that sometimes getting more sleep is simply not an option. You may be working two jobs, you may be caring for young kids and elderly parents, or you may not have enough control of your schedule. Get through it the best you can and when you finally do get some free time – prioritize your sleep! Also, look for other quick opportunities to recharge your battery. Try breathing exercises, yoga, reading, meditation, or a short walk. Any activity that gives you a chance to rest and reset in the short-term will only help you in the long run.

TRY THIS

How much sleep did you get last night? Was it enough? How do you feel about your health, productivity, and relationships today? Could they be improved if you invested more time sleeping or recharging?

READ MORE

The Time Paradox
A Perfectly Productive Day
Managing Your Energy

YOUR LISTS

---

*To-do lists help us
break life into small steps.*

Randy Pausch

YOUR LISTS

Love them or hate them, everyone seems to have a very strong opinion about lists.

Some swear by them. Some swear at them. Some are prodigious list makers. Others just dream about having them. Lists can be a life saver or a pain in the rear end. They come in all sizes and shapes and live in all sorts of places. I have seen people write lists on sticky notes, random scraps of paper, or even on their hands or arms.

No matter how you feel about them, one thing is indisputable. Writing lists is a much more effective way to remember and keep track of things than relying on our brains. While our brains are hard-working and very good at a large number of activities, from running our bodies, to creative thinking, to problem solving, they are not very reliable storage centers.

Although I do most of the grocery shopping, every so often my husband will be heading to the store and will ask me what I need. I will rattle off a few items and he'll rush out the door. When he gets back I'm lucky if he's brought back three out of five of the requested items. When I go to the store and ask him what he needs, those items immediately get added to my shopping list and my success rate is almost always 100%. Now, instead of asking him to get a few items for me, it's much easier for me to just add them to my shopping list.

If you want to remember something, especially over a period of time, your best bet is to write it down. There are literally hundreds of types of lists you can make and maintain. In the next few chapters, we'll examine a variety of lists you can use to help you get more organized, increase your productivity, and make sure nothing falls through the cracks.

Keep in mind that the true beauty of lists isn't in making them, but rather in what you do with them on a daily basis. Crafting and then cultivating your lists is the only way to derive true value from them.

9
YOUR LIFE IN LISTS

Richard Branson, founder of Virgin Group and author, disclosed on his blog that the secret to success is to "write it down."[3] He shares, "Ever since I was a child I have made lists of all kinds, including short-term tasks, long-term goals, and resolutions. It's how I make sense of the world, bring order to the ideas in my head, and start turning them into action."

I believe him. I have lists for everything. It's how I have been able to keep everything in order and stay on top of everything for many years. The real key to success isn't just about writing it down but also how you organize and manage your lists.

Here are some ideas of some lists you can create and maintain to help you keep everything in order. We'll evaluate each of these in detail in the upcoming chapters.

SHOPPING LISTS

Keep lists of everything you need to buy. I organize mine by store, so when I'm in that store, I pull up its corresponding list. A great app for this is AnyList which allows you to share your shopping lists. You can also order the categories according to the layout of the store to make sure you don't inadvertently miss something on your list.

WORK LISTS

If you are an individual contributor working on a number of projects, organize your lists by project. Include everything from tasks, to open questions, and items you need to follow up on. If you are a manager, organize your lists by employee. Again, include all open items. I use a notebook that I always keep with me so I can write things down as soon as they come up. For team projects, KanbanFlow is another great tool to keep track of tasks.

TASK LISTS

The key here: only have one to-do list for all the things you have to get done and make sure you always have it with you. Most people I talk to have lists in all different places, their work notebook, their phone, sticky notes, and in their head. When it comes down to it, items get forgotten or fall through the cracks.

ENTERTAINMENT LISTS

I keep lists of books I want to read, shows I want to watch, movies I want to see, restaurants I want to try, places I want to visit, and people I want to catch up with, so whenever I have some free time I can quickly scan through my lists and find something to do. I keep most of these lists in the Notes section of my phone so I can access them quickly from anywhere. And I use GoodReads to keep track of the books I have read and the ones I want to read and I get great recommendations as well!

DONE LISTS

I am a strong believer in documenting completed tasks and accomplishments because it makes you feel good and motivates you to do more. I have kept a "Done" list in various forms for over twenty years. It also serves as a great reference if you need to look back on when something happened or names of people you may have met with in the past or when asking for a raise at work.

If you want to learn more about how lists can help you become more productive, check out Paula Rizzo's book, *Listful Thinking*. It's an easy read. If you want to have some fun with lists, you can try *Listography: Your Life in Lists*, a series of journals of different lists.

> **TRY THIS**
>
> What lists do you currently maintain? Which work for you and which ones don't? What lists might be helpful for you to have? What's the best format for each one of your lists and where should you keep them to ensure they are readily available when needed?

> **READ MORE**
>
> Enjoy Happier Holidays with Lists
> Cultivating Your Lists
> Achieve Balance By Maximizing Your Tools

THE MAGIC OF A SINGLE TO-DO LIST

Approximately 80% of us use some sort of calendar to manage and keep track of our time. We diligently log our meetings, appointments, birthdays, and other reminders. However, surprisingly, I also found that 80% of us do not have a consistent system or methodology for tracking our tasks. Hmm.

Much has been written and debated about whether or not you need a to-do list. Based on my informal polling research, only 12% of people say they regularly keep and maintain one centralized list of all their tasks. The rest either keep everything in their heads or maintain many, many scattered lists and notes.

Some of us jot down tasks on a scrap piece of paper when we remember something we need to do, but this list ends up being incomplete. Some may use a notebook or try to remember tasks by adding notes or reminders on our phones. Others hope that somehow it will all just get done.

As a life-long maker and maintainer of a to-do list, I can attest to the value of establishing and maintaining one single list of all of your tasks. It can be paper, digital, or you can use a task management app. It doesn't matter where you keep your list so long as you maintain one list that's always right at your fingertips.

Here are some of the magical benefits of having a single to-do list.

FREE UP YOUR MIND

There are a million random thoughts running through your head on any given day. By writing down all your tasks, you can relieve your mind from having to remember everything and free up space to do the important work of creative thinking and problem solving.

YOUR TASKS HAVE A HOME

If you have one list, you have a no-brainer place to store all your tasks. You don't need to keep a variety of lists, reminders, or random sticky notes. Instead, you will have created a place to house everything you need to remember to do. And, you will no longer need to keep reminding yourself to remember to get something done. The list will do it for you.

IT'S HANDY

For the magic to work most effectively, you really need to keep your list with you at all times. If it's on a piece of paper on your desk, when you get a new task or remember something you need to do, you won't have it with you. And more likely than not, you won't remember it when you're back at your desk. Also, if it's with you, it's much easier to check off items as you complete them, which saves you from having to take time to update your list.

YOU'LL FEEL GREAT

The real magic of having a to-do list is the pleasure that comes with checking off completed tasks. I have been known to add items to my list that are already done just to be able to tick them off. It's a proven fact, that checking items off a list results in a dopamine rush, which makes us feel good and in turn, motivates us to do more.

> ### TRY THIS
>
> Where do you keep track of all of your tasks? In your head? On various pieces of paper? In your phone? Which place works best? Pick one place and create one central list and make sure all of your tasks are included. Keep it with you at all times so as things come up, you can immediately add them to the list so they don't fall through the cracks.

> ### READ MORE
>
> Cultivating Your Lists
> The Prioritization Puzzle
> The Most Important Tasks

11

THE PERFECT TO-DO LIST IS A PRIORITIZED ONE

So, you've created a centralized to-do list, now what?

Most of us want to get everything done as soon as possible. In this rush, we often avoid prioritizing tasks and instead jump right into picking the easiest of them to tackle. After all, why waste time managing or prioritizing the work when you can get right to tackling them?

Let's start with a simple statement: all tasks are not created equal. Some are easy to finish and others may take weeks or months to complete. Some may be fun and enjoyable while others are a real drag. Also, they all don't have the same impact. Some of the tasks we complete can have a dramatic and significant impact while others may go unnoticed.

Let's be honest, having to choose what to prioritize is challenging and many of us don't know where to begin. There's an entire chapter later in the book on how to prioritize your tasks based on importance and urgency but, for now, let's first understand why prioritizing your list is just as important as having a list.

YOU CAN'T DO IT ALL

Don't try to get everything done all at once. Many people give up on their to-do lists because they become too overwhelming. While the list should contain everything you need or want to get done, you need to prioritize your most important daily tasks so it's more manageable and achievable and you don't feel deflated.

YOU ULTIMATELY DECIDE

If you don't proactively and deliberately choose how to spend your time, you'll spend your time on the things that come your way but may not be the best use of your time or your attention. How many times are you nearing the end of the day and you can't figure out where the time went? What did you get done? As Jim Rohn reminds us:

> "Either you run the day or the day runs you."

YOU STAY FOCUSED

It's much easier to think about or follow up on a few things at a time versus trying to do a little bit on a lot of different things. Imagine ten balls in front of you and you have to push them all over the finish line ten feet ahead of you. What if you try to push each one a little at a time? Or, what if you kick them to the finish line one ball at a time. Which option do you think will get them all over the finish line the fastest?

I once worked with a colleague who always prioritized the most recent task. So whatever item was most recently discussed became the most important thing to work on. Very quickly we found that priorities kept changing and we all had a hard time completing any one task before another one took precedence. Moreover, as we worked really hard to keep up with the new incoming requests, the projects that required more time, focus, and effort kept getting pushed to the bottom of the list. In time, we realized that while we were doing a lot, we weren't necessarily focusing on the most important or impactful work.

Keep in mind, Author Karen Martin's famous quote:

> "When everything is a priority, nothing is a priority."

TRY THIS

Think about what you need to get done. What if you proactively picked a few of these items to focus on instead of trying to tackle them all at once? Do you have a sense of which tasks you should address first? Is it easy for you to prioritize or is it a struggle?

READ MORE

Cultivating Your Lists
The Fallacy of Doing It All
The Prioritization Puzzle

12

THE MOST IMPORTANT TASKS

So, we have a to-do list and things get added to the list but now what? While most of us know the value of creating and updating our lists, many of us don't really know the best way to manage it once we have one.

Most productivity gurus promote the concept of selecting a few tasks to focus on at a time instead of trying to do everything all at once. Leo Babauta, author of *Essential Zen Habits*, popularized the term the Most Important Task (MIT) to promote the idea of identifying your top one to three tasks each day.

In one of his fascinating episodes of the *Pinkcast*, a podcast focused on delivering productivity tips and tricks in 2 minutes, Daniel Pink asserts that using the MIT process is a simple trick to getting the right stuff done. He encourages you to write down your MIT and do it first. He writes his MIT down on a piece of paper on his desk and also on the whiteboard on the wall right in front of his computer. He takes this hack very seriously![4]

For me, it's a little like playing Tic Tac Toe. Each day I pick my top three priorities and focus my time and efforts on making sure they get done. I win whenever I get three tasks completed before the end of the day. Sounds easy and fun, right?

To help me make sure I do this everyday, I baked this feature right into my task management app, priorigami.

Each day the app sends me a notification to select my "Daily Top Three." I set my reminder for 8 a.m. each morning but you can choose to receive your notification at a time that works best for you.

I click on the notification to review my list of tasks and then I simply drag and drop my "Most Important Tasks" into the "Daily Top Three" section. The app tracks my progress and sends me an update towards the end of the day serving as a nudge to finish up any remaining tasks.

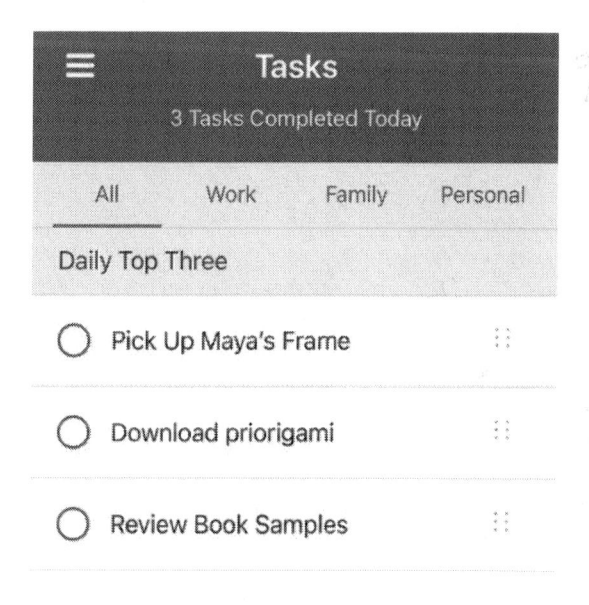

☰	Tasks		
	3 Tasks Completed Today		
All	Work	Family	Personal

Daily Top Three

○ Pick Up Maya's Frame

○ Download priorigami

○ Review Book Samples

Undoubtedly, things come up and priorities change during the day so you can always go into the app and reprioritize your "Daily Top Three" tasks if needed. Even on days you're able to stay on track, it's a good habit to review your list throughout the day.

Since I tend to get distracted during the day, I added a notification alert in priorigami that reminds me to review and shuffle my MITs at 2 p.m. each day. More often than not, I find myself working on tasks outside of my top three so this little reminder helps me get back on track and forces me to reprioritize if needed.

The best part is that the app congratulates me each day I complete all three MITs.

TRY THIS

What are the Most Important Tasks on your list? If you had to pick one to three items to prioritize for tomorrow, what would they be? Throughout the next day, focus on your MITs checking on your progress periodically and consider if and how you need to adjust your focus or your priorities.

READ MORE

The Magic of a Single To-Do List
Cultivating Your Lists
The Juggling Act

13

THE LINGERING TASK

What's the most troubling aspect of maintaining a to-do list? It's often that annoying task that has made its permanent home on your list and never gets checked off. When you break it down, there are really only a few reasons why certain tasks linger longer than others.

Here are a few ways you can get rid of those sticky tasks.

JUST DO IT!

Some tasks are important but for whatever reason, we just don't want to do them. We procrastinate and avoid the task altogether. However, sometimes a small mindset shift can help us finally make progress on that item that has been hanging on our to-do list – much like a strong odor that remains long after you've taken the trash out!

Often, the most challenging part is getting started. Once we actually get going, we find that it isn't as difficult or as bad as we had anticipated. Remember, the first step is often the hardest.

DELETE IT!

Successfully maintaining a to-do list is not just about completing items but making decisions about what should and shouldn't go on the list. Sometimes you add a task to your list with good intentions of getting it done, but over time it lingers because it's really not that important. In that case, it should be removed from your list. If it's important enough, you can always add it back at a later time.

BREAK IT DOWN!

Other tasks stay on your list because they may feel too big or too overwhelming to tackle. In this case, break it down by creating subtasks. For example, a task like "Plan the Party" is too daunting. Instead, create more digestible tasks like:

- Set Date for the Party
- Create Guest List
- Draft Party Invitation
- Select Menu

When I was thinking about taking an international vacation, I realized my passport was about to expire so I added a task to my list to renew it. After a few weeks, I noticed that it was still on my list and I hadn't made any progress against it. I realized then that the task itself was too big, intimidating, and overwhelming so I never prioritized doing it. After all, who wants to renew their passport?

I deleted that task and added a new first step: "Get Passport Renewal Form." That was much easier for me to stomach. Once I got the application, I added a task to complete the application and then another to take my passport photo. By breaking it down into several simple steps, I was able to renew my passport in time for our vacation.

You'll find that you will have much more success getting larger projects done by listing out and completing more manageable tasks. Another example, instead of creating a task to "Get a New Job," start with "Update my Resume."

TRY THIS

Look at your to-do list and review the tasks that have been on your list for more time than you'd like to admit. First, decide which ones you can delete. Then, break down the tasks that are too large. Finally, determine if it's important enough to make it a top priority for tomorrow and get it done so you can check it off your list once and for all!

READ MORE

The Constraints of Procrastination
Cultivating Your Lists
The Two-Minute Rule

14

THE "TO-DON'T" LIST

There's a lot of talk about our to-do lists, but have you ever heard about the "to-don't" list? Fran Hauser, an executive coach, author, and speaker, first wrote about it in her book, *Embrace the Work, Love Your Career*.[5]

She makes the point that it's just as important to clearly identify the things you aren't going to do as it is to choose the things that you are. Let that sink in.

To help you focus on what's most important, consider making a list of all the things you could do, or have been asked to do, but shouldn't because they'll take up your time and attention without bringing you closer to achieving your goals. Put these things on a separate "to-don't" list.

Once I started doing this, I realized a few things. First, it became much easier for me to say "no" to doing certain things because I had predetermined that those tasks weren't strategic and weren't worth the distraction.

Also, I found I was able to put the things on my "to-don't" list out of my mind and not waste any mental energy contemplating them. It was almost a relief to have made a clear and definitive decision to not focus on those things. I found that it gave me permission to put those items aside and not worry about them at all. Out of sight, out of mind.

This practice also helped me feel less overwhelmed when I had too much to do.

Recently, when looking over my calendar, I took note of the time I was spending on women's networking events and mentoring. While I am very passionate about advancing women in the workplace and coaching and encouraging women, I realized that the amount of time I was spending wasn't in line with some of my other goals. I added not taking on any new mentees or accepting event requests to my "to-don't" list and it became much easier for me to set this boundary.

The good news is that like any other list, the things on this particular list do not have to stay there forever. In fact, you should get in the habit of reviewing the list periodically to determine what should stay and what else could be added.

TRY THIS

Are there things that you spend time on that aren't helping you achieve your goals? Would it help for you to add it to your own "to-don't" list? What other activities are taking up a lot of your time or that could be added to this list? Consider how having a "to-don't" list could help you set and stick to your boundaries.

READ MORE

The Myth of Time Management
Less is More
The Juggling Act

15

THE "DONE" LIST

Several articles have been written about the value of keeping a "done" list as a key motivator and driver of increased productivity. Some people track daily accomplishments and then move on, others keep an active spreadsheet listing everything they have completed. Others choose to focus on their three big goals and track progress against those goals.

When I first started working and was especially proud of my accomplishments, I kept a weekly list of what I had achieved. I would email this "status report" to my manager at the end of the week to share the progress I had made. At first, I wanted to give an update, but in time, I realized these lists also highlighted the contributions I was making to my team and to the company as well.

Later in my career, I switched to an annual list of major successes. At the start of each new year, I'd eagerly create my new list and anticipate how it would get filled in over the next twelve months. Every few weeks, I'd go in and update it.

Here are some of the categories I like to track:

- Product Launches
- Blog Posts
- Research
- Business Books Read
- Influencer Outreach
- Networking
- Training & Development

- Agreements and Contracts
- Community Service

Over the years the categories shifted and morphed based on where I was working and what I was focused on achieving that particular year. The key is to keep track of the things that are most meaningful and important to you in terms of achievement. Think about how you define your own success and how you would measure it.

Not only does the "done" list serve as a motivator, it documents my achievements for future reference. It certainly helped me when I had to write my annual self-assessments. Even years later, I have gone back to my lists to confirm key product launch dates. I have been able to quickly find out which training courses or assessments I completed in order to make a recommendation to someone else. I have also gone back to find names of people in my network so we could reconnect. These lists have become an incredible historical repository that I find myself referring back to time and time again, especially since as I age I can no longer rely solely on my memory.

As I was pondering writing this book, Jeff Hilimire shared in his newsletter that he had founded a publishing company and was interested in hearing from wanna-be authors. I remembered that somewhere along the way, Jeff and I had met and had a fabulous conversation about productivity hacks and priorigami. I was able to go back to my "done" lists and noted that indeed we had met in 2017. Recalling this meeting made it much easier for me to reach out to him and to reference our connection.

One might conclude that this book might not exist if it weren't for my "done" list!

TRY THIS

What did you accomplish today? Write it down. What did you get done this week? Write it down. How do you feel? Are you amazed by what you were actually able to get done? Or, do you feel you didn't get enough done? How would you measure your productivity or success based on what you achieved?

Use the answers to these questions to help you design a format and a system for your own "done" list.

READ MORE

The Importance of Why

16

THE "SOMEDAY" LIST

We all can and should dream. Dreams make fairy tale futures come true. Big dreams help us strive for and achieve more. They are visionary, inspirational, and motivational. But sometimes, these big dreams also get in the way of our short-term wins.

When I look at to-do lists, they seem to be a mix of quick, small wins, urgent follow-ups and some big, hairy, audacious goals (BHAGs for short). One of the challenges of managing your to-do list is that the tasks aren't created equally. Some are easy and within your control while others require several steps and rely on others to do their part. Others require time or money that we may not have.

So, we tend to prioritize the quick wins, even if they aren't as important or impactful. While these tasks should be on your list and prioritized, what about those things that aren't as urgent but may still be very important?

The "someday" list is the list of your dreams. It's a list of all the things you want to do but probably aren't going to do today, tomorrow, or in the next week. But they are still valid and deserve a home on a list. The "someday" list is my favorite list. It's the most hopeful and least stress-inducing list.

Want to write an article, book, or a screenplay? Want to take a dream vacation? How about that home renovation project you've been thinking about? Or starting your own business or buying a new home? All of these are legitimate tasks and goals, but they clog up your to-do list and distract you from focusing on the most immediate tasks at hand.

Some call this a "bucket list" or a "parking lot." It doesn't really matter what you call it, just that you create one. It's also a great way to capture all those ideas so you don't lose sight of them.

Over the years some of the things that have been on my "someday" list have included:

- Becoming a Naturalized U.S. Citizen
- Hot Air Ballooning
- Visiting Hawaii
- Learning How to Paint (as in art, not walls)
- Writing a Book
- Getting a Patent
- Starting my Own Business
- Renovating my Kitchen
- Planting a Vegetable Garden
- Digitizing my Old Photos
- Going on a Safari

And there have been many others. Some I've achieved. Some have fallen off the list, and some are still on the list hoping to be realized at some point in the future.

One of the items from my "someday" list that became a reality was getting a patent. While many inventors aspire to acquire a patent to protect their intellectual property, many are intimidated by the process. Also, the average time to get a patent is several years at best.

When I was at The Weather Channel, we were innovating in the digital media space and hired someone to oversee our U.S. patent program. He was able to break down the deliverables and usher us through the arduous process of submitting several technology patent applications. As a result, between 2007 and 2014, I was awarded four different patents for my inventions including a formulation for calculating and determining the best times to do certain activities through a Climate-Based Activity Index, a desktop software framework, and a searchable message board.

When it comes time for you to tackle one of the items from your "someday" list, remember to break it down into actionable tasks and add a few at a time to your to-do list. You'll find it much easier to check them off your list and slowly but surely, make progress against your dream goal. Keep in mind, taking the first step is often the most difficult of them all.

TRY THIS

Look at your to-do list. Are there some lofty goals on there that you haven't made any progress toward? Would they be good candidates for your "someday" list? Maybe you've been dreaming about something big – a home project, a new job, or an exotic vacation?

Start your "someday" list today so you don't lose sight of your dreams.

READ MORE

Cultivating Your Lists
Make SMARTer Resolutions
Bringing Your Vision to Life

17

ENJOY HAPPIER HOLIDAYS WITH LISTS

Each year, it feels like we barely get through Thanksgiving and suddenly the rest of the holiday season looms before us. While this is a time for joy, togetherness, and happiness, it's also a source of immense stress. The expectations of the holiday season have become so overwhelming and there's a limited amount of time to get it all done. No wonder it seems to start earlier each year. So, how do you survive the season?

Not surprisingly, I manage to keep on top of it all with a whole bunch of lists that I keep year after year to help me stay organized. After all, Santa makes his list and checks it twice, so why not give it a try?

And before you say, "A whole bunch of lists, I thought we needed just one to-do list," let me clarify.

You should have one centralized to-do list. Period. But often, a task may necessitate the creation of supporting lists, some of my own found below. For example, on my to-do list I may add a task to "Send out Holiday Cards," but in order to do so, I need to create a subsequent list of recipients.

Below are some of my supporting lists that I use to complete tasks throughout the season.

HOLIDAY CARD LIST

For years, I have maintained a holiday card list of all friends and family members I want to keep in touch with. It includes their mailing addresses for easy reference along with a record of cards that we have sent or received. As cards come in, I update names of new family members or new addresses for those who have moved. Throughout the year, I reference this list whenever I need a mailing address.

WISH LIST

I have been told repeatedly that I'm really hard to shop for. For the most part, I have more than I need and don't have a long list of wants. Recently I realized that by creating my wish list I could make it easier for my family members (and reduce the number of returns to deal with after the fact).

GIFT LIST

I create a gift list, organized by each individual. I try to note where I might buy the present and any other details such as size or color. It's been nice to look back and see what gifts I've purchased in years past so I don't repeat anything. It also ensures that I haven't missed anyone.

HOLIDAY PARTY INVITE LIST

The holidays are a great time to get everyone together and I am a big fan of the seasonal holiday gathering. I start from last year's invite list and then over a week or so, add names as I think of people or run into them. This process helps me make sure I don't overlook anyone and invite new friends as well.

HOLIDAY MENU SHOPPING LIST

Two weeks out, I plan the full menu for all holiday meals. I list out all meals, number of guests, and which dishes I plan to make. Then, I use this list for creating the grocery list and the meal prep timeline. Doing this ahead of time allows me to determine which items can be bought in bulk or the farmer's market versus the neighborhood grocery store. Also, I can figure out which items can be prepared ahead of time versus just in time.

> **TRY THIS**
>
> What makes you most anxious about the holidays? Take time to create some of these supporting lists to help you get organized. How do you feel? Does it help relieve some of the stress by writing it all down?

> **READ MORE**
>
> Your Life in Lists
> Cultivating Your Lists

18

CULTIVATING YOUR LISTS

We've explored four primary lists you should be keeping for better personal and professional management: the "to-do" list, the "to-don't" list, the "done" list, and the "someday" list. We also discussed the occasional offshoot list... a list resulting from a task on your "to-do" list such as groceries for the task of making a holiday dinner.

Now that we're clear on the types of lists you should be keeping, I must share that making lists is just the start. Creating a list is an easy first step, but the reality is that making a list is simply not enough – maintaining it is the ultimate key to success.

Frankly, culling down your to-do list is almost more important than creating one. The most effective lists are active and reviewed daily. You excitedly check off the tasks that you've completed. You proactively prioritize your most important tasks. You remove the ones that have been lingering too long. You break down the ones you don't tackle because they are too overwhelming. And, you add new tasks as soon as they come up.

Cultivating your list is an art and a skill that requires discipline and practice. It sounds like a lot of work. Maybe it will be at first, but as you get used to doing it, it becomes an easy and indispensable process.

Think of it like planting a garden. To see the fruits of your labor (literally), you must first prepare the bed then plant your seeds. And much like your list, this is just the beginning. You cannot expect the seeds to bear fruit without tending to them after they've been sown.

In addition to the right amount of sunlight, they need to be watered, pruned, fertilized, and cut back. And, even when they grow and bear fruit, they need to be harvested. The truth is that the ongoing care and feeding is more critical than the initial planting. Candidly, there's no point in planting the seeds if you're not committed to the time and effort that is required for their ongoing care. The same is true for your lists.

When I was in college, I thought it would be cool to get a plant. Yes, just one little corn plant. How hard could it be to keep it alive? Just some sunlight and water, right? It was exciting at first but then I got busy and forgot about it, and it inevitably died. Similarly, unattended lists die. But, with focused attention and ongoing cultivation, they will thrive.

TRY THIS

Where's your to-do list? When was the last time you reviewed it? You may need to dust it off or create a new one if you can't find it. First, quickly review it and mark the tasks you've completed and delete the ones that are no longer relevant. Add in important tasks that aren't already on the list. Finally, prioritize the top three most important ones. Do it again tomorrow.

READ MORE

The Magic of a Single To-Do List
The Perfect To-Do List is a Prioritized One
The Most Important Tasks

YOUR STUFF

---

*Fill your life with experiences, not things.
Have stories to tell, not stuff to show.*

Abhysheq Shukla

YOUR STUFF

We love our stuff. We love to buy new stuff. Collect stuff. Save stuff. The more stuff, the better, right? Usually, this is hardly the case. What is the tipping point when having too much gets in the way of getting stuff done? And, how much of all this stuff is actually useful?

Have you ever done an inventory of your wardrobe? Research shows that most of us only regularly wear 20% of the items in our closet. 80% is taking up space and collecting dust. Try storing the clothes you actively wear in a separate section or try turning the hangers around for easy identification. Within a few weeks, you will clearly see which items you wear and which ones could be donated, recycled, or discarded. If I try on something and it doesn't make me feel fabulous, I immediately put it in my giveaway bin, not back on the hanger.

When was the last time you went through your pantry? Somehow, whenever I finally get around to cleaning it out, I find that at least one-third of the "non-perishable" items have expired. Clearly, I need to do this more often! I hate to even ask when you last thought about all the stuff in your basement, attic, or storage unit.

The reality is that it's so much easier for us to gather and collect stuff than it is to determine what's actually valuable and purge what isn't being used. My parents lived in their home for over forty years and while a lot of things were brought into the house, not many ever came back out.

Don't get me wrong, there's absolutely nothing wrong with collecting items you love—if you're enjoying them. The question to ask yourself is what value does each item provide and how can you extract the maximum utility from everything you own and the tools you use?

The goal is to get the most out of everything we have.

In the following chapters, we'll consider different ways to manage your possessions and identify ways to fully leverage the tools you use. There are so many ways to organize to make your life simpler.

A PLACE FOR EVERYTHING

Most of us have way too much stuff and managing all of this stuff takes up way too much of our time. And let's not forget, looking for things negatively impacts our time and productivity. How often do you find yourself wandering around the house looking for your keys, your phone, or your wallet?

There's a simple, but not easy, solution. Take a full inventory of all your stuff and establish a set place for everything you own.

Do you have a junk drawer, desk, or corner in your house? Most likely it's because these random items don't have a home. Sort through and categorize them and then allocate a location, box, or folder for each. For example, select a location for your keys and your phone, find a place to store your bills until they get paid and another for after they've been paid, and pick a specific place for your work bag or purse.

When my son went to college and moved into his first apartment, I bought him a wooden bowl for the kitchen counter. The idea was to create a central place for him to put his keys, wallet, and anything else from his pockets as soon as he got home so he could easily grab them as he headed back out. For all the things that have come and gone with every move he still has the wooden bowl on his kitchen counter.

If organizing your stuff feels too overwhelming, it's probably because you have too much of it. If you haven't used it, worn it or thought about it in six months, then get rid of it. I know it's hard to part ways with your things but if you aren't using it, wouldn't it feel great if someone else could?

Think about it. Most of us don't have rubbish lying around because by habit, we put it in the trash can for easy removal. Likewise, create bins, bags, or spaces for things you need to return, things you want to try to sell or things you want to donate.

Once everything has a home, you need a process to maintain it... think of it as housekeeping. For some, you'll get in the habit of automatically putting everything back in its place. Others may need to set aside time each day or week to put things away. And then there are some who will wait until you have visitors, maybe even resorting to paying house cleaners. I try to do a quarterly purge similar to trimming the bushes or getting a haircut.

TRY THIS

Start with one room. Take a look around and inventory your stuff. What do you use frequently? Are those things easily accessible? Which things did you forget you had? Do you still need them? What about the items that are cluttering the space? Can they be moved?

No matter which process you prefer to follow, when your stuff has a home, you will waste less time looking for it.

READ MORE

Less is More
The Three-Bin System

20

LESS IS MORE

In his book, *Essentialism: The Disciplined Pursuit of Less*, Greg McKeown explains, "Essentialism is not about how to get more things done; it's about how to get the right things done." He continues, "Sometimes what you don't do is just as important as what you do."[6]

While we've already examined how this concept relates to our lists, this concept is not just limited to our tasks. Let's examine several different ways this simple concept can also apply to how we manage our stuff, our time, and digital distractions as well.

As we consider how to become more productive, we need to think about how much we have in our lives and how to handle it all. The volume of what we are trying to tackle can feel overwhelming. So, what if we limit the number of things in our life? Sounds a bit backwards, but the easiest way to become more productive is to reduce the number of things we are juggling.

I was fascinated by the story of Robin Greenfield, a twenty-nine-year-old entrepreneur, environmental activist, and minimalist who has limited his possessions to just 111 items that fit in his backpack. In a blog post from 2016, he wrote, "Through my years of downsizing, I've found that material possessions don't create long-term happiness or fulfillment for me. I've found that an overabundance of possessions hinders my purpose and passion rather than facilitates it."[7]

In a subsequent post written in 2020, Robin had limited

the number of items in his backpack down to just forty-four items! He shared, "The possessions I do have serve a purpose, allowing me to live simply and sustainably, meeting my basic needs and helping me to inspire others to live in harmony with our earth, our global humanity and all species."[8]

This concept applies to the amount of time spent as well. Recent research and experiments have proven that working fewer hours results in increased productivity as well. In fact, in 2000 the French government mandated a 35-hour work week and has also since eliminated checking email after hours.[9] Several companies in Sweden have experimented with a 6-hour work day and found that they did just as much, if not more, than they accomplished in 8 hours by working more efficiently.[10] Other studies conducted in the United Kingdom have shown that companies that reduced their work week to 4 days instead of 5 actually demonstrated consistently increased productivity and business performance.[11]

Possessing too much *stuff* applies to our technology as well. Nowadays, there is an app for anything and everything imaginable. According to Techreport's Mobile App Download Statistics from 2023, the average phone has over eighty apps installed, even though many of them are not actively used.[12] Not only are they taking up storage space on your phone, they also get in the way of your efficiency.

At one point, I had accumulated over six screens full of apps. There were some apps I didn't remember downloading and others I didn't even recognize. I found that whenever I went to do something specific on my phone, I would have to scroll through various screens to find the app I was seeking. (I know, I know... I could just use the search feature). In my quest to find said app, I would inevitably get distracted by some other notification. Ultimately, as a result of the diversion, I would forget which app I was trying to access in the first place!

One day I finally decided to clean up my act. First, I removed all of the apps I wasn't using including those I didn't recognize or remember downloading. Then, I moved all of the apps I use infrequently to the last few screens and put all of the apps that I use the most on my home screen.

Now, I only have to go to one screen to do most of the things I want to do. It also helped to create folders (such as tickets, travel, banking, etc.) for similar apps to make the most of my screen real estate. Trust me, taking the time to do this every few months will save you a lot of time in the long run.

What are some of the things that may be cluttering up your life or getting in your way? Think critically and deliberately about focusing on the Most Important Things you have. The old adage, "Less is More" proves that by focusing on less, you have more time, energy, and attention to give to the things that matter most.

TRY THIS

You too can become an essentialist. Simply ask yourself, "What things around me are cluttering up my life and not adding value to it?" Challenge yourself to focus on the few, rather than the many, and start by eliminating distractions and time wasters.

READ MORE

A Place for Everything
The Value of Being Organized
The Three-Bin System

THE THREE-BIN SYSTEM

It bears repeating that we all love our stuff. We especially love getting new stuff. New clothes, shoes, books, furniture, decorations, household items, you name it. It's almost impossible not to want more when we are constantly bombarded by ads of new and innovative things that we "need" and "want." In fact, consumerism is at an all-time high.

Over time, we realize that slowly but surely, we've collected a ton of stuff. And, while it's easy to bring things into the house, how often are we taking things out of the house? Probably not frequently enough.

Most of us are diligent about removing trash from our homes, not only because it's hygienic but also because we have a process and a schedule in place. We have trash cans in every room and we know that garbage pick-up falls on certain days. We have a similar process for recycling, sorting packaging, and materials and bringing them out to the curb on a regular schedule.

What if we did the same for our other stuff? Here's how I implemented the "three-bin system" to help me create a process and schedule for purging all the other things that collect in the house over the years.

TO RETURN

I have an area in our mudroom, near the side door, that I use most frequently for items that need to be returned, replaced, or fixed. It serves as a nice visual reminder as I'm coming and going, so that if I have an extra 30 minutes that day, I'll grab the item on my way out and make a stop at that store.

TO DONATE

I have several bins in various closets throughout the house for donating used household items. As I see items I haven't used or clothes I haven't worn in a long time that could benefit someone else, I immediately put them in the bin. Once a quarter, I take the items to the donation center.

TO SELL/RECYCLE

Then there's the stuff that you no longer need, but can't get rid of. Maybe the item is too valuable to give away or perhaps it's not something that can be discarded with the garbage. This stuff tends to hang around the most and takes the most effort to purge.

Think about old electronics – how many old phones are completely useless but are still hanging around? What about the outdated jewelry you never wear anymore? Next time you have a free afternoon, gather up a few of these items and take them to a consignment shop or post them for sale on a trusted online marketplace.

You may even make some extra spending money. And, of course, with that extra cash, you can go out and buy more stuff! (Or maybe you shouldn't if you're intrigued by the idea of becoming an essentialist!)

TRY THIS

Look at the room around you. What do you see? What are the things you enjoy and use and what are some of the things that you've forgotten about that are cluttering up your space? Which bin would you put them in?

READ MORE

A Place for Everything
Less is More

22
THE SHOPPING LIST

The most commonly used list is the food shopping list but it's also one of the most ineffective. How many times do we go to the grocery store only to leave the store realizing we forgot something or even several things? How many times do we come home from a trip to the grocery store only to find we've forgotten three or more items? Or, as soon as we get home from the store a family member casually mentions something that they now need that wasn't even on the list.

If you're like my family, you go through food quickly and spend a lot of time at the grocery store so creating, maintaining, and using a great shopping list is an incredible time saver. The first step is to make sure you have a shopping list. Only one. I repeat, just one grocery shopping list.

Second, create a process for adding things to your list as soon as you realize you need something. The easiest thing to do is to update your list as soon as you finish something in real-time, when you're looking in the fridge, or during downtime while cooking.

Finally, find an easy way for your family members to add things to the list. There are a number of shopping list apps that make it simple to collaborate with other members of your household. However, if your family is anything like mine, you may have to resort to the old-fashioned way of asking them for their needs right before going to the store.

For years, I have used an app called AnyList to keep track of my grocery list. It's free, simple to use, and has some cool features including the ability to add ingredients to your shopping list from recipes. For me, the most useful feature is that the app allows you to categorize your items by department (bakery, deli, meats, produce) and even more helpful is that you can move the categories to follow the layout of your grocery store of choice!

I cannot tell you how easy it is for me to walk through the store and gather the items that I need from my list in the same order they appear. This one feature alone has saved me time and trips back to the store. Now, instead of running around in different directions like a rat stuck in a maze, I make a beeline straight for the checkout line.

If apps aren't your thing, you can do the same thing on paper. Categorize your shopping list by department and store layout.

I also create individual lists for each store I frequent. I have a different list for Target, Costco, and Trader Joe's for example. Anytime I'm heading out to a store, I quickly review the list, add any missing items and then reference it as I'm shopping.

As I'm walking through the store, I often wonder if people think I'm distracted by emails or texts when in reality I'm just going through my shopping list and deleting items as I pick them up. As I do this, I think about those people walking through the store without any list at all or with scraps of paper and wonder how many items they are going to forget.

TRY THIS

How do you manage your grocery list? Is it working for you? What could you do differently to make sure you get everything you need while spending as little time as possible in the store? How much time would you save if your list was organized according to the layout of your grocery store?

READ MORE

You Life in Lists
Cultivating Your Lists
Achieve Balance By Maximizing Your Tools

23

ACHIEVE BALANCE BY MAXIMIZING YOUR TOOLS

So many of us strive to achieve the elusive ideal of work-life balance. We relentlessly pursue the ultimate alignment of work, family, and personal goals which proves challenging given the finite number of hours we have each day. So, is this desire even realistic or is it a myth?

I certainly have not mastered the art of balancing it all – or more accurately, juggling it all. At times, I've been so overwhelmed I've given in to the imbalance. When I'm just trying to get through each day and not making time for my self-care, I get irritable, tired, and I don't sleep well which makes it all that much worse the next day.

I learned the hard way that not making time for myself, my health, and my well-being to focus on short-term to-dos really isn't in my best interest, or, for that matter, for any of those around me. Now, when I start to feel testy, grumpy, or impatient, I take a time out to reset my priorities. I now see these symptoms as a notification or alert to myself to prioritize self-care.

Here's how I take advantage of my tools to help me find some semblance of balance in my life.

YOUR TO-DO LIST

I adopted a few techniques to help me prioritize family

and personal tasks above all the work tasks. To begin, I now categorize my tasks by Work, Family, and Personal and I try to make sure there are always a few things in the Personal section. On the weekends, I prioritize the Personal items over the Work items to make sure I'm spending time on me.

YOUR CALENDAR

I color-code all meetings and appointments so I can visually see where I am spending my time. I have assigned specific colors for work meetings, family activities, exercise, and fun social activities.

Once a month, I try to zoom out to take a look at the entire month. Of course, there are weeks when one or two colors seem to dominate, but when I have the flexibility, I schedule more time for family and personal activities. The more colorful my calendar is, the more I know I am doing a better job of balancing my time.

Time	Mon	Tue	Wed	Thu	Fri	Sat	Sun
7 am	7-8 Fall Break	7-8 Fall Break	7-8 Fall Break	7-8 Cleaners			
8 am		8-9:30 PAWS Ed Session	8-10 9th Grade Fall Coffee	9-9:30 Walk with Kathryne	8-9 Social Media Post	8-9:30 Yoga	8-12 State Baseball Tournament
9 am					9-11:30 Google Ads		
10 am	10-11:30 Haircuts	8-9:30 Walk with Jen	10-4 Launch Day	10- Huddle		9:30-11:30 Tutor	
11 am		11- #MondayMotive		11-1 HUG Meeting			
12 pm		11:30-1 Lunch with Maya				11:30-1:30 Lunch with Marc	
1 pm		1-2 Publish Blog Post		1-2 Webinar			12:30-4 Play
2 pm		2-4 Website Walk Through		2-4 Customer Feedback Review	1:30-2:30 Plan Banquet		
3 pm					2:30-3:30 Call Ron	2:30-3:30 Pick up kids	
4 pm	4-5 Game	4-6 Football Practice	4-6 Football Practice	4-6 Football Practice	4-7:30 Football Game		
5 pm							
6 pm			6-9 Volleyball Playoffs				
7 pm						7-10:30 Varsity Game	7-11 Concert

YOUR TEAM

If you're working on a bigger project or planning an event with a team of people, it becomes even more challenging to keep track of it all. I use KanbanFlow for work and personal projects to create task cards, prioritize them, assign owners, and set deadlines. You can color code the tasks, alert collaborators when new tasks are assigned, and set reminders for approaching deadlines. There's a free version and it's super simple for anyone to use.

YOUR FRIENDS

When work tasks get overwhelming, it's easy to skip some of the personal or family activities. To avoid doing this, I make a habit of scheduling these activities with a friend. It's much harder to cancel when you've coordinated doing something with someone else.

This is especially true for me when it comes to walking or exercising or going out for lunch or dinner. Not only do I make sure I'm making time for relaxing and enjoyable activities for myself, but I get the bonus of catching up with a friend.

> **TRY THIS**
>
> Look over your to-do list or calendar to assess if you're balancing all the different demands on your time. Is there something that's taking up a lot of your time? Are there things you wish you were doing but aren't? Which of these techniques could help you achieve more balance in your day-to-day life?

> **READ MORE**
>
> The Magic of a Single To-Do List
> One Balanced Life to Live
> Just Say No!

24

I FORGOT MY PHONE... AND I SURVIVED

We carry around our smartphones as if they were a part of our body and check them an average of eighty-five times a day. Not only do they serve as phones, they have replaced calendars, cameras, alarm clocks, and radios. For some, they have even taken the place of computers. Makes you wonder what would happen if we forgot it one day.

One morning I was up, ready, and out on time. I was feeling good and confident despite the drizzly weather. Then, I realized I forgot my phone. Panic set in. My heart rate picked up and I tried to think through whether I had enough time to go back and get it. I didn't.

Right then, I realized how silly my reaction was and decided I was going to see how I fared without it. Could I do it? The first few minutes were full of angst as I wondered about missed calls or texts that would be waiting for me. I thought about being completely unreachable and unable to follow up immediately. Nevertheless, I pushed on, determined to somehow make it through the day.

As I thought ahead, I realized I also didn't have my calendar. I would have to go from memory until I could get to my computer. I wondered about the rain and reached for my phone to check the weather. Nothing there. I would just have to plan for the worst case and prepare.

At my first meeting, I got a new "to-do" and instinctively reached for my phone to add the task to my list. Ugh. Again, no phone. Oh well. I would have to try to remember to add it to my list later.

For the first few hours, I found myself feeling restless as I felt for my phone in my back pocket out of habit. Even though I knew it wasn't there, I was still reaching for it. Wishful thinking?

Throughout the day, without my phone and its distractions, I was able to engage more in my conversations which proved to be quite enjoyable.

Without my phone, I didn't check any social media sites but I also didn't miss out on any big news or events either. And while my email messages certainly piled up more quickly, digging out wasn't as overwhelming or as time-consuming as I had imagined.

In fact, productivity experts claim it's more efficient to look at emails periodically versus checking constantly. If only I could stick to this school of thought.

I certainly didn't miss any of the dinging sounds of alerts, notifications, or reminders. And, not only was I not distracted by these, but I didn't forget anything either. I realized that other real-world triggers were sufficiently effective in helping me remember the important things that needed attention.

As the day went on, the less I missed my phone and the less I reached for it. I finally relaxed and felt at ease. I could do everything I really needed and most importantly, I survived the day without any incidents or negative impacts.

Since the day of my unintended "experiment," I've been more aware of the research studies confirming the addictive nature of smartphones as well as the negative effects of prolonged screen time. In fact, what I experienced could be classified as mild symptoms of "detoxing." While I felt anxious and nervous at the start of the day, I actually started to feel much better towards the end of it.

While we've come to rely on our smartphones to do a lot of the heavy-lifting for us, we should keep in mind that there is a point where they cause more anxiety and less fulfillment.

Honestly, I hope I forget my phone at home more often.

TRY THIS

You know what I'm going to suggest and I also know you're shaking your head. So, just think about it. How about putting your phone in the other room for an hour or so? How about taking a walk or attending a meeting without it? Once you've taken that smaller step, try leaving it at home for a longer period.

How does it feel? Can you survive without it? Chances are, you might find that you are more present and less distracted.

READ MORE

Five Productivity Pitfalls
Managing Your Energy

PRODUCTIVE PACKING FOR YOUR NEXT TRIP

How many times have you gone on vacation and realized you had forgotten something? Happens to my husband all the time. He has forgotten his belt, sunglasses, swimsuit, medications, and even his wallet. At this point it's a family joke and we all try to guess what he might forget on our next trip.

Here are some simple tricks you can use to make sure you remember everything you need so you can enjoy your trip without the worry of not having something you need.

For starters, don't wait until the very last minute to pack.

KEEP THE ESSENTIALS

Keep the essentials that you need for every trip in a bag that's ready to go at any time. Include the necessities like a sewing kit, first aid kit, basic medicines, and toiletries. Then, it's a no-brainer and time-saver to quickly grab and pack it whenever you're heading out on a trip.

VISUALIZE YOUR TRIP

Think through and visualize your trip. Imagine yourself going through each day. What are you doing? What will the weather be like? How many times will you need to change clothes? What gear or accessories will you need? How many nice or casual outfits will you need? Try to picture yourself there and walk through the entire trip in your mind to clearly see what you will need to bring along with you.

MAKE A LIST

About a week before your trip, start making a list of all the things that you will need to take, focusing mostly on the one-off items that you don't use every day. Good examples are chargers, reading materials, travel documents, loyalty cards, and accessories (depending on your destination). Also, remember all travel documents and access to travel and reservation confirmations and addresses. Reference this list as you begin packing.

DO A DRY RUN

The day before your trip, pack your toiletries in your travel case and then use it the morning of your trip. Make sure everything you need comes out of your travel bag. By doing this, you will quickly realize if you've forgotten something and you can immediately add it to your bag and then you're good to go.

The good news is that if you do end up forgetting something, you'll be able to purchase it from a nearby store. My husband has amassed quite an impressive collection of logoed resortwear!

TRY THIS

What have you forgotten to pack on previous trips? Would any of these practices have helped you remember that item? Before your next vacation, visualize your trip, make a list of the must-haves, and try to do a dry run the morning of your trip.

READ MORE

Arrive on Time Every Time
The Constraints of Procrastination
Always Have a Plan "B"

YOUR DAY

---

*Don't count every hour in the day.
Make every hour in the day count.*

Alfred Binet

YOUR DAY

Each day we're given 24 hours, 1,440 minutes or 86,400 seconds. That seems like a lot and also never enough. While the amount of time we have each day doesn't change, what we get out of it varies greatly. The key is to figure out how you can maximize each and every day without burning yourself out.

At some point in my early years, Benjamin Franklin's quote was imprinted into my brain:

"Never leave till tomorrow that which you can do today."

I came to believe that the key to my success was to finish everything on my to-do list each and every day. At the end of each day, I would run around trying to check off those last few tasks before going to bed. It was exhausting and ineffective. Instead of feeling fulfilled at the end of each day, I became tired and frustrated, thinking I still didn't get enough done, and worried there was too much left to do the next day.

I had to rewire my brain to accept that getting everything done in a day was simply not an achievable goal. I had to learn to set more realistic expectations for myself, starting with planning each day. I began taking 5 to 10 minutes at the beginning of each day (some may prefer to do it the night before) to plan how I would tackle the day's to-dos.

We'll dig further into different ways to do this in the upcoming chapters, but I start by looking at my calendar to see how much time is already scheduled versus how much is available for accomplishing the next tasks on my list. Next, I take my top three daily tasks and work them in with the goal of tackling the hardest and most challenging of tasks first. And, as ridiculous as it may sound, blocking off time for relaxing, socializing, or recovery activities pays dividends.

By planning my day according to the time I have, I found that my daily goals became more reasonable. And, I replaced Benjamin Franklin's words with Scarlett O'Hara's conclusion at the end of *Gone with the Wind:*

> "After all, tomorrow is another day."

26

START EACH DAY BY MAKING YOUR BED

I have always made my bed first thing in the morning. I don't think about it. I just do it and have done so every single day for years. It's become part of my daily routine. I don't see it as a chore or a waste of time, but as my first simple win of the day. In fact, I still make my half of the bed even if my husband is still sleeping in it.

However, no matter how hard I try, I cannot convince my kids to make their beds! They don't see the value in it. To them, making the bed is a waste of time since it'll just get messed up again. When my daughter was a college student studying psychology, she explained that she simply doesn't get the dopamine rush from making her bed like I do. So, why should she bother?

Well, research reported in *Psychology Today* shows that "bed makers are happier and more successful than those who don't."[13] In 2014, Naval SEAL Admiral McRaven included the following remarks in his commencement address at The University of Texas at Austin:[14]

> If you make your bed every morning you will have accomplished the first task of the day. It will give you a small sense of pride, and it will encourage you to do another task and another and another. By the end of the day, that one task completed will have turned into many tasks completed. Making your bed will also reinforce the fact that little things in

life matter. If you can't do the little things right, you will never do the big things right.

And, if by chance you have a miserable day, you will come home to a bed that is made — that you made — and a made bed gives you encouragement that tomorrow will be better.

If you want to change the world, start off by making your bed.

As proof, 66% of my Facebook friends say they make their beds every morning to feel good and get their day started off on the right foot. Many also commented on how good it feels to get into a made bed at the end of the day.

To make it easier to make your bed each day, get rid of extra pillows and cushions, remove the middle flat sheet or just use a duvet and simply pull it up. Believe it or not there's now a Smartduvet that comes with a phone app that will automatically make the bed for you. This magical duvet blows air through a technology layer so the crumpled up duvet automatically smooths itself out. I'm not entirely sure that this counts as making your bed, but perhaps I should order this for my kids so they start on the right foot with the push of a button.

TRY THIS

If you don't normally make your bed, try it for a few days in a row and see how it impacts your day and how you feel. If you typically make your bed, try not making it for a few days, how do you feel? Do you notice a difference?

READ MORE

A Perfectly Productive Day
Eat that Frog
Don't Break the Chain

27

A PERFECTLY PRODUCTIVE DAY

One no-brainer way to increase your productivity and sanity is to perfectly plan out your day to ensure you do the most important things when you are most focused and energetic.

To get started, spend a week assessing your focus and energy levels throughout the day so you can identify your finest hours for deep work. During this time, keep a notebook handy and log when you are able to focus and be productive versus the times when you are restless, unfocused, or lack energy.

According to my focus and energy levels, this is how my typical day unfolds. First, I need some "me" time in the morning and then my most focused and productive time of the day is between 8:00 and 10:30 a.m. After that, I begin to lose focus. By noon, I need some social interaction, movement, and external stimulation. Afternoons are my most unfocused and low-energy times and then I get my second wind in the late afternoon to early evening. After that spurt, I need time to wind down.

7 am	Gearing Up Time
8 am	Focused Quiet Time
9 am	
10 am	Unfocused Time
11 am	
12 pm	Social Networking Lunch Time
1 pm	
2 pm	Unfocused Time
3 pm	Low Energy Down Time
4 pm	
5 pm	High Energy Active Time
6 pm	
7 pm	
8 pm	Gearing Down Time
9 pm	

It doesn't really matter how your energy levels rise and fall through the day, what's helpful is recognizing your natural highs and lows.

Once I understood how my energy levels ebb and flow throughout the day, I was able to clearly determine the best times for certain activities or tasks resulting in optimal efficiency. Through this exercise, I decided to reorganize my schedule to focus on deep work versus checking email first thing in the morning. For many years, I had started my day pouring through and responding to emails before realizing I was actually wasting my most productive hours doing mindless work.

Here's what my perfectly productive day should look like:

Time	Block	Time	Task
7 am	Gearing Up Time	7 am	Yoga/Tea/Breakfast
8 am	Focused Quiet Time	8 am	Read News/Articles
9 am		9 am	Write Blog Post/Articles
10 am		10 am	Check Email
11 am	Unfocused Time	11 am	Make Phone Calls
12 pm	Social Networking Lunch Time	12 pm	Lunch Meeting
1 pm		1 pm	Check Email
2 pm	Unfocused Time	2 pm	Scheduled Meeting Time
3 pm	Low Energy Down Time	3 pm	Watch Webinar/Podcast
4 pm		4 pm	Email and Social Media
5 pm	High Energy Active Time	5 pm	Kids Sporting Event or Exercise
6 pm		6 pm	
7 pm		7 pm	Dinner
8 pm	Gearing Down Time	8 pm	Watch a TV Show
9 pm		9 pm	Read a Book

In the column on the right, I've schedule my daily tasks according to the energy level blocks shown on the left. While this presents the ideal case for me, inevitably things come up that prevent me from sticking to my optimal schedule. That said, starting with a solid framework helps me structure my day when I do have some flexibility.

My mother was a very successful and accomplished Director at the Smithsonian Institution as well as the founder and President and Executive Director of her own non-profit organization, Global Performing Arts. Although she managed, her natural clock didn't conform to the expectations of the modern working world since her most creative and productive hours were later in the evening. However, now that she is retired she can finally work her schedule around her high-energy periods late into the night and take her time in the mornings to enjoy some quiet time while sipping her tea.

TRY THIS

Track your energy and attention levels throughout the day for a week. Evaluate your high- and low-energy times and look for patterns. Create a framework for your perfectly productive day and see if you can re-order some of your activities to take advantage of these high-energy periods.

READ MORE

The Myth of Time Management
The Time Paradox
Managing Your Energy

28

EAT THAT FROG

I have never liked the name of this productivity concept. But it's incredibly simple, memorable, and, more importantly, it works. This technique stemmed from Author Mark Twain's famous quote:

> "Eat a live frog first thing in the morning, and nothing worse will happen to you the rest of the day."

The resulting time management strategy was popularized by Brian Tracy in his book, *Eat That Frog!: 21 Great Ways to Stop Procrastinating and Get More Done in Less Time*.[15] At the heart of this approach is to identify one challenging and important task you need to get done that day. Resist the inclination to pick the easiest or quickest one, and instead think about the most impactful task and do it first.

The magic of this methodology is that once you've "eaten the frog," not only do you feel a sense of accomplishment earlier, but everything after that appears much simpler to tackle. If you procrastinate you'll have that daunting task hanging over your head all day, weighing you down. And, guess what? You'll still have to get it done before the end of the day when you're tired, lacking focus, and in a rush.

Here are three ways this method sets you up for a productive and successful day, every day.

FORCED FOCUS

By setting aside time for a specific task, you are giving yourself permission to eliminate distractions. When you're focused on a task at hand, you are not distracted by notifications, texts, or emails that can be addressed later. Also, focused time ahead of time will result in better work.

YOU'RE SET FOR SUCCESS

Once you've accomplished your big task, you won't have to worry about it for the rest of the day. We feel good when we get something done, which motivates us to keep up the momentum throughout the remainder of the day. If you wait until the last minute, you may not feel as energized, motivated, or creative.

IT'S SIMPLE

This is probably the simplest productivity tip you can integrate into your life. It doesn't require a lot of planning ahead and it's easily repeatable. In fact, it's so easy, it's hard not to at least give it a try.

As I have mentioned, I used to start my day checking and responding to emails and before I knew it, it was mid-morning and I felt like I hadn't accomplished anything substantial. I also realized that I wasn't doing the most valuable work during the time my brain was most energized and focused. Instead, I do a quick scan of my emails to make sure there's nothing urgent and then switch to my most important task of the day.

TRY THIS

What one big thing do you need to get done tomorrow? Instead of hoping it'll get done, look at your calendar and schedule a block of time earlier in the day to get it done. How did you feel once it was done? How did you feel for the rest of the day?

READ MORE

It's All About Time Blocking
The Constraints of Procrastination
The Most Important Tasks

GO WITH THE FLOW

Although I try to plan everything in advance and adhere to my schedule, everything doesn't always go according to my best-laid plans. This is especially true when it comes to creative thinking, brainstorming, and writing. Unfortunately, ideas don't come pouring out on demand. No matter how much I would love to control this, I have learned to accept that when it flows, you must embrace it. And, when it doesn't, you have to take a step back and try again at another time.

For example, I try to play Spelling Bee almost every day – throughout the day, as time permits. In this game, you try to make as many words as possible from seven random letters, including one central letter. As I get started, the words flow out easily. But at some point, they stop coming. Oftentimes, especially on weekends, I keep at it long after the momentum has gone. However, when I'm not being stubborn, I've come to learn that if I step away, and come back to it after some time, I can quickly find a few more words.

People often share that ideas come to them in strange places including while walking, falling asleep, or even in the middle of the night. When ideas would come to me at these non-traditional times, I used to try to ignore them or remember them for a more convenient window. However, I would often completely forget about them or what I remembered wasn't as good as my original thoughts.

Instead, I now force myself to go with the flow. When these thoughts and ideas start coming, I stop what I'm doing and take advantage of the moment. This includes getting out of bed and grabbing my laptop or taking 15 minutes after my walk to get my thoughts down on paper. If something comes to mind while you're driving you can send yourself a voice message that you can later transcribe. Even though this could be seen as disruptive, I find benefit in embracing these moments of creativity.

The good news is your schedule is not rigid. You can move things around. And, as I shared in the "Double or Nothing" chapter, if you already scheduled a backup period, you automatically have another opportunity to tackle that task later. It proves more challenging when your task involves someone else, but depending on who you are meeting, it could be OK to ask for a 15-minute grace period to keep your momentum.

On the other hand, if you schedule time for a creative task and you find yourself staring into space, make yourself stop. It's frustrating to feel like you're giving up or giving in, but time not well spent is wasted. After 10 minutes, if you haven't broken through your block, look at your calendar and see if you can move things around to revisit the task later in the day. If that's not possible, allow yourself a quick break and come back to it. Even stepping away for a few minutes can get your creative juices flowing again.

Try this technique when brainstorming, problem solving, and puzzles too! The best way to get ideas flowing again is not to force it.

TRY THIS

Next time you're stuck on a creative exercise and the ideas just aren't flowing, take a short break or move things around on your schedule to revisit it at another time. If your head is swirling with thoughts and ideas, stop what you're doing and get them out of your mind and write them down somewhere you can reference later.

READ MORE

Double or Nothing
The Power of a Shower

THE POWER OF A SHOWER

At one point or another, we have all struggled with writer's block or fixated on a problem with a seemingly impossible solution. We may find ourselves obsessing over a disagreement with a friend or a comment we made that could have been taken the wrong way. Maybe we're anxiety ridden about an upcoming event, project, or deliverable that we're not sure how we're going to get done.

During these times, we naturally tend to focus more of our time and energy on the issue or concern versus distancing ourselves from the problem itself to reassess. During especially challenging times, I take a step back by taking a shower. You heard that right, a shower. Sounds weird, doesn't it?

John Kounios, professor of psychology at Drexel University and co-author of the book *The Eureka Factor: Aha Moments, Creative Insight, and the Brain* explains that while you're in the shower you achieve a perfect balance of engagement and disengagement that boosts innovative thinking. This allows your subconscious mind to think creatively about the problem at hand and come up with some new ideas or solutions. Taking a shower is also relaxing which releases dopamine which in turn unleashes your creativity.[16]

Those of us who are hyper-focused on getting things done might see taking a shower as a waste of time. I used to jump in and jump right out to get on with my day. I have since reframed my thinking to recognize that taking my time in the shower actually helps me in several ways. First, it helps me relax and recharge. It also increases my productivity by giving me time to gather my thoughts and come up with new ideas or solutions. I now see this as critical planning time for the rest of my day.

For me, a shower works best when I'm not trying to solve a specific problem and can let my mind wander freely. During these times, I have come up with catchy headlines, responses to difficult situations, cool gift ideas for loved ones, and even some of the themes for the chapters in this book. I am often pleasantly surprised to see where my thoughts take me during this unstructured time.

Of course, if you're at the office, you can't jump in the shower, but taking a short walk or break to read an article or play a game can have similar effects. Whenever you are stuck on a problem or can't seem to find the right words, find a different activity that is both distracting and relaxing.

TRY THIS

Next time you find yourself obsessing over something, take a break. Whether it's a shower or a walk, do something mindless and watch how the ideas and thoughts start to flow.

READ MORE

Sleep is Not Wasted Time
Go With the Flow
Getting Over Feeling Overwhelmed

31

THE TWO-MINUTE RULE

This rule is simple in theory but hard to put into practice. Yet, if you can get in the habit of doing it, I promise it will save you time.

The concept was first introduced by David Allen in *Getting Things Done* and many productivity experts continue to promote it, including Daniel Pink in one of his Pinkcast episodes.[17]

Here's how it works: If you can complete a task in less than two minutes, you should just do it. Don't put it off, don't try to remember to do it later, don't even write it down. Just do it and get it done. Simple.

Here are some examples that might help put this approach into context.

When you bring in the mail, stand by the recycling bin and go through it. Immediately throw out any junk mail. Sort your bills into a pile to batch pay later. File anything that you might need to keep or reference later. Create a "follow up" pile for anything left over.

Similarly, you can use this rule for going through your email. This methodology, called Inbox Zero, is rooted in the same principle. Set aside time-specific slots throughout your day to check email and then follow these steps:

1. Delete junk immediately.
2. Archive or file emails that you may need to keep and refer to later.
3. Forward emails that can be delegated.
4. If a response or action can be done in under two minutes, just do it.
5. The rest require further action and should be managed as action items.

Other opportunities to save time include putting your clothes away as you change, washing your dishes after eating, and making your bed as soon as you get up in the morning. Imagine never having to find time to wash a whole pile of dishes or clean your room or closet. You also won't ever have to spend time looking for your favorite sweater.

You can also use this rule in other ways as well. Take two minutes to call your Mom, text a friend, or thank someone who did something nice for you. These are the types of things we think about doing but never get around to. How often do you hear yourself say, "I was going to call you or text you, but I've been so busy?"

Instead of putting it off, just do it as soon as you think of it. Not only does it accomplish the task, but you feel good and so does the recipient of your kind thought.

TRY THIS

As you go through the rest of your day, challenge yourself to immediately tackle anything that can be completed in less than two minutes. At the end of the day, assess how it went and how you felt. Did you get more done?

READ MORE

The Constraints of Procrastination
The Lingering Task
The Prioritization Puzzle

32

SO MANY INBOXES, SO MUCH WASTED TIME

My phone buzzes. My instinct is to grab it to see what's needed, but where do I check first? With so many incoming messages across so many different inboxes, how do we keep up?

We waste so much time checking and responding to messages without realizing how ineffectively we are using these tools to communicate.

So, back to my phone. I read a few text messages and respond to one. Move on to email. I have a personal and business email both with an overwhelming amount of messages – I'll come back to that point later. I have ten messages on my Slack channel, something must be going on. My LinkedIn app is showing notifications of people who want to connect. Facebook Messenger is alerting me to incoming messages and unread posts. I have new likes on Twitter, Instagram DMs, and the list continues.

Exhausted yet?

An hour later, what have I actually accomplished? Absolutely nothing. And quite honestly I'm not sure what I've learned and what I should do next. It's like flipping through 200 TV channels without watching a thing.

Here are some communication best practices organized by channel you should keep in mind before sending your next message.

TEXT MESSAGES

Unless you're communicating with close friends or family, reserve texting for short, urgent messages that can be addressed with a short response back. Try to avoid sending group texts keeping in mind that every response goes to all recipients. Also, try not to open up discussions on text that would be better served through a phone call or a meeting.

EMAIL

Use email for most communications to share information, coordinate meetings and events, or collaborate on ideas. Email is also great for communicating with groups of people. Use email if you're asking the recipient to do something for you. This way your message will also serve as a reminder to them. Like with text messages, use the "reply all" function only when your response will benefit all recipients on the messaging chain.

SLACK/MICROSOFT TEAMS

These are both effective ways for teams to communicate and collaborate virtually. However, with the onslaught of messages, it's easy to lose track of action items or find information for future reference. Try pinning or flagging messages that you want to come back to later.

FACEBOOK

Facebook is a personal, social network and should be used to communicate primarily with friends and family.

Be thoughtful about reaching out to colleagues since they may not be comfortable connecting on a personal level. Similarly, you never know if an employer may stumble across your social media down the line so share wisely. Also, be mindful about how you promote your products or services. Instead of a hard-hitting direct pitch, wrap a soft sell in a meaningful personal anecdote or story.

LINKEDIN

Think of LinkedIn as your extended professional network. This is where you can connect comfortably with work associates and partners. Be sure to limit posts, messages, and updates to professional topics and articles. Avoid expressing personal political or religious opinions.

INSTAGRAM

People look at Instagram, they don't read it. The photo or image you post should be the message and should stand alone. People shouldn't have to read captions and comments to understand the message.

More importantly, you don't need to send out the same message across all channels. Pick the most appropriate communication channel for your message and send it!

For birthdays, I get phone calls, voice mails, text messages, What'sApp notifications, Facebook posts and messages, and LinkedIn posts and messages all day long. While I'm sincerely thankful for each of these messages, it's a lot of places to keep up with. When I want to wish someone congratulations or a happy birthday, I pick one platform – the one that I use the most to connect with that person.

Gotta go. My phone just buzzed. It must be something urgent.

> **TRY THIS**
>
> Set aside times throughout the day to check your various inboxes. To stay focused, I find it helps to turn off all notifications, alerts, and badges that could cause a distraction. Before you send your next message, think about the best practices above and make sure you're using the best channel for the message and the recipient too.

> **READ MORE**
>
> Less is More
> Achieve Balance By Maximizing Your Tools
> Five Productivity Pitfalls

ARRIVE ON TIME EVERY TIME

At the end of summer, kids head back to school and anxiety seems to increase as pressure mounts due to the madness of the morning rush. How many of us start our mornings with, "Hurry up! We're going to be late!" With the same morning routine and commute, why is it so hard to be on time? It's not as if the school's start time or destination changes from day to day. Yet in spite of this, too often making it to school on time, from the minute the alarm goes off to saying goodbye in the carpool line, seems to be just as impossible as running a marathon in record-breaking time.

With all the tools and technologies in our repertoires, from fancy alarm clocks to GPS apps to Amazon's Alexa or Apple's Siri, we don't have any excuses for being late.

Here are some of the techniques I use to help me arrive on time.

GRAB AND GO

Make sure you have everything you need to take with you ready before it's time to leave. It's critical to make sure there's a place for everything and that everything is in its place so you are not hunting for your car keys or looking for lost shoes when it's time to leave.

Find a set place for your keys and create a "mudroom" space somewhere for shoes, coats, hats, and backpacks. With the kids, I encourage them to gather all their stuff the night before so they aren't scrambling in the morning.

BUFFER TIME

Before you leave, even if you know where you're going, check your Maps app to see how long it will take to get there and ensure you're taking the best route – especially if you live in a metropolitan area with unpredictable traffic congestion. This will help you anticipate and avoid unforeseen trouble spots. Take the time that is projected and add 20%. For example, if it says it'll take 10 minutes, give yourself at least 12 minutes to get there. For a 20-minute drive, leave 25 minutes ahead of time.

For meetings, leave your office with enough time to get to the conference room by the time the meeting is scheduled to start. If necessary, leave enough time to stop by the restroom or check in with a co-worker.

HAVE A PLAN

If you are going somewhere you haven't been, do your research. First, check and review the directions. Find out where to park and how long it may take to walk to your destination from the lot. Keep the phone number or contact information of the place or person you're meeting on hand in case you get lost or need more detailed directions.

Don't worry about being too early. Take a few extra minutes to check email or social media, make a quick phone call or, even better, review and update your to-do list! It's also a treat to spend a few quiet minutes sipping coffee, stretching, breathing, or relaxing.

Regardless of what techniques they use, some people are chronically late. It could be ingrained in their personality or maybe they take a different approach to time management. In these cases, more extreme measures may be needed such as changing clocks 15 minutes ahead or finding accountability partners to help them keep track of time.

TRY THIS

Next time you are running late, think about whether any of these approaches would have helped you arrive on time. Before you head out, give one of these tips try and see if it helps you manage your time better. If you find something that works, make it part of your routine.

READ MORE

A Place for Everything
Productive Packing for Your Next Trip
Always Have a Plan "B"

34

MAKING MEETINGS WORK AGAIN

I hate meetings. There, I said it. It's out there. Mostly I hate meetings because the vast majority are an utter waste of everyone's time.

According to Pumble's *Meeting Statistics You Should Know* in 2024, employees spend approximately 31 hours in unproductive meetings each month. In a survey of 5,000 workers conducted by Atlassian, 72% of the meetings we attend are ineffective. Which is the reason so many of us find ourselves asking, "Could this meeting have been an email?"[18]

So many of us spend hours and hours in meeting rooms talking and discussing without a clear objective. We don't really know why we are there, what we are supposed to do, and what should happen after the meeting – except to schedule yet another meeting.

Meetings are one of the most unproductive elements of our day but they don't have to be. With some discipline, meetings can be quite efficient and effective, and dare I say, even quite satisfying.

Here are some easy ways to make your meetings work for everyone.

- Schedule meetings in advance and think critically about the amount of time that's needed. Most can be handled in 15 to 30 minutes.

- Be thoughtful about who is invited to attend and what their specific role is in the meeting. Try hard to limit the number of attendees and remember you only need to invite one person to represent each department or group.
- Set a clear objective for the meeting. Identify and communicate the specific goal and expected outcome of the meeting prior to the meeting.
- Outline an agenda including topics with time allocations and send it to meeting participants in advance so they are prepared.
- Start meetings on time and end early to allow people time to regroup and get to their next meeting on time. Let everyone know that this is your plan – they will appreciate your consideration, will be less likely to multitask and may even help you keep on topic.
- Identify a record keeper to take notes, document decisions and record action items which should be assigned to specific people with deadlines.
- Ensure the discussion and all comments stay on topic and are relevant. If other topics arise, suggest scheduling a separate time to discuss them and encourage everyone to keep on track as respect for everyone's time.
- As soon as the meeting ends, add any action items you may have been assigned to your to-do list so you don't forget about them.
- Send meeting notes to meeting participants within 24 hours of the meeting including key decisions, action items, and next steps. Schedule any follow-up meetings if needed.

TRY THIS

Before you schedule your next meeting, stop and review this list. Pick one or two of these suggestions to implement and see how it works and what reaction you get. Keep what works and throw out what doesn't. Then pick a few more to test for your next meeting.

No matter your job title, you can become a leader and a role model in your organization by leading your own effective meetings.

READ MORE

Making the Most of Your Time
Arrive on Time Every Time
The Three List Assessment

THE FALLACY OF DOING IT ALL

As I've already mentioned, this book was born out of the question: "How do you do it all?"

Yet, in going through this process, it became crystal clear that I don't do it all. The reality is that we simply cannot do it all, no matter how much we want to or how hard we may try. I may do "a lot" relative to others, but there's no physical way to do it all. So, why even try? And, how did this even become a requisite of success?

Trying to "do it all" leaves us exhausted, frustrated, burned out, and feeling as if we've failed. It is striving for an unattainable goal. Would we try to walk to the moon? Would we set a goal to swim across the Atlantic Ocean? Would we try to read every book ever written? Or count every star in the night sky? No, because these are not reasonable expectations and neither is trying to do everything.

What if we reframed this aspiration to focus simply on doing all the things that truly matter? How would that shift your perspective or change your stress level? Even as I am writing this sentence, I felt an immediate sense of relief.

The key to living productively and efficiently is to stop trying to do it all and instead focus on ensuring we're doing the right things. This is why prioritizing is so critical. It forces us to take a hard look at what's most important to achieve our goals.

This is much easier said than done though. When forcing yourself to prioritize, it helps to keep these three realities in mind.

YOU CAN'T SAY YES TO EVERYTHING

What would happen if you accepted every invitation, watched every show, tried to become best friends with every person you ever met, or ate everything at the all-you-can-eat buffet?

Imagine piling up your plate with every option on the buffet. Not only would your plate be overflowing, but if you ate everything you'd end up feeling very uncomfortable afterward. Instead, as we go through the buffet, we pick and choose certain foods over others to fill our plates satisfactorily. Apply this same lens to the things that fill your time.

FINDING BALANCE IS EVERYTHING

Just as you can't exclusively eat meats, carbs, or sweets, you need a balance of activities in your day as well. You can't do it all, but you also shouldn't just do one thing either. You can't work all the time without a break or on the flip side, you can't just watch TV all day either. Try to find the right mix.

BURNOUT LEAVES YOU NOWHERE

If you're running yourself into the ground getting it all done, you are likely negatively impacting your physical and mental wellbeing and the relationships with those around you. There's little reward in getting everything done at the cost of losing yourself.

TRY THIS

Look at your to-do list and your calendar. What's on there that shouldn't be? Get rid of them. Going forward, before you take on a new task, volunteer, or say yes to something new, consider whether it's something that really matters. And remember, you can't do it all.

READ MORE

Achieve Balance By Maximizing Your Tools
One Balanced Life to Live
The Prioritization Puzzle

YOUR LIFE

---

*Life isn't about waiting for
the storm to pass,
it's about learning to dance
in the rain.*

Vivian Greene

YOUR LIFE

Life is funny. We expect a lot out of it but we don't give it much thought. Sometimes it feels like life is just what happens to us. And as we're focusing on trying to make the most of each day, the years somehow continue to pass us by.

I believe that life doesn't just happen to us but it's what we make of it. It takes work and effort but we do get out of life what we put into it. I've shared a lot about managing the small stuff and now we'll turn to ways to figure out the bigger picture.

So, how can you take control of your life and live the life you want? It starts with clearly analyzing, evaluating, and identifying what you want out of your life. This can take many forms. You may consider developing a strategic plan for your life. Some of us choose to make annual resolutions. Or, you could simply identify a yearly theme. In the coming chapters, we'll consider different ways to do this.

No matter how you choose to surface or visualize the life you want, you must learn how to prioritize and focus on the "things that really matter" or the most important things. I'll share a variety of unique ways you can organize or think about how you want to tackle tasks to ensure you're living the life you want. Again, there are no right or wrong ways to do this – just the ones that make sense and work for you.

Recently, I began harboring feelings of a mid-life crisis and I'm starting to worry that I'm running out of time to do all of the things on my bucket list. So I decided to prioritize "experiences." I started by listing out some of the unique things I wanted to experience like hot air ballooning, glass blowing, wine making, etc. Then I decided to schedule one a month to knock off twelve items in a year. It's working. I've done so many new things and feel like I'm living my life to the fullest.

If you're wondering if looking at life deliberately is worth the time and the effort, remember Ferris Bueller's wise words:

> "Life moves pretty fast. If you don't stop and look around once in a while, you could miss it."

ONE BALANCED LIFE TO LIVE

Throughout this book, I've been sharing different ways to categorize, dissect, segment, and prioritize different aspects of our lives. We attempt to create and use these divisions to figure out how to get it all done while staying sane. We spend countless hours trying to achieve the perfect balance between conflicting demands on our time and attention.

How often do you think and talk about work-life balance? Work-life balance is one of the most critical factors employees consider when evaluating a new job opportunity. According to Hubstaff's *Work-Life Balance Statistics* for 2024, while 72% of US workers believe work-life balance is a crucial factor, 60% share that they don't have boundaries between work and life responsibilities. In third place behind compensation and career opportunities, 78% of US workers report that they would change jobs for better work-life balance.[19]

As I mentioned earlier, at one point in my career, I was completely out of balance. I wasn't doing enough at work or for my family, let alone ever doing anything for myself. I honestly believed that achieving the mythical "work-life balance" was simply not possible. I had even created a pie chart of time spent on various activities in an attempt to equalize time spent on work, family, and myself. You guessed it, that didn't work.

So, I decided that instead I would reframe the problem. I gave up trying to balance conflicting demands and started thinking about the pie as a whole. I stopped thinking about the contrived compartments of my life and thought about the big picture. After all, we all just have one life to live.

Now, instead of worrying about the amount of time spent at work or with family, each day I prioritize the top three most important things – regardless of what category they fall within. In the big picture, does it even matter? What really matters is making sure you're getting the most important things done.

Some days all three tasks are related to work, some days it's a mix and honestly some days all three priorities are about my life. Over time I began to realize that if I took care of the things in my life, I would also be more productive at work. In fact, the days when my family or personal tasks were out of whack, I couldn't focus on or deliver my best work anyway.

This mindset shift literally changed my life. My one life. Now, instead of the unrelenting tug and pull, this holistic view allows me focus and harmony.

More importantly, as a manager, I expect my colleagues to do the same. I encourage them to prioritize caring for their sick child, taking a mental health day, or tending to a pressing issue at home. Not only do they appreciate the relief from the pressure they feel, but most work harder and deliver better results when the weight of those burdens have been lifted.

TRY THIS

Does your life feel balanced? If not, where do you feel the most pressure? Prioritize addressing some of those areas of your life to alleviate the stress. Does it really matter if they are personal or work-related? For brownie points, have you prioritized doing something for yourself today?

READ MORE

Achieve Balance By Maximizing Your Tools
The Fallacy of Doing it All
Managing Your Energy

MAKE SMARTER RESOLUTIONS

We spend so much time worrying about all the little things that need our attention. The start of a new year is a great time to think about the big picture.

Every year, on January 1 we all get another chance at a fresh start. According to Forbes, 45% of us set New Year's Resolutions hoping a bit of accountability will help us achieve our goals in the year ahead. So, does this tradition actually work?

Forbes reported that while only 8% of those who made resolutions succeed in fully achieving them, people who explicitly make resolutions are ten times more likely to attain their goals than people who don't make any resolutions at all.[20] So, why not give it a try in the coming year?

First, think about one, and only one, overarching thing you would like to improve, change, or accomplish next year. Any more than one is a sure fire way to fail because change is hard and when the going gets tough it's easy to want to give up.

In general, some of the most popular resolutions people make are to:

1. Lose Weight
2. Save Money
3. Change Careers
4. Quit a Bad Habit
5. Spend More Time with Family and Friends

One year, I wanted to focus on embracing change. Another year I decided to work on becoming a better listener. You may want to become more productive or patient or achieve a specific goal like writing a book or launching a new product. Perhaps you want to lose weight or eat healthier, save money, or read more.

One common aspect of these themes is that they are grand, overarching, and ambiguous. You will be a lot more successful if you set SMART goals. When setting a SMART goal, simply make sure it is:

Specific
Measurable
Attainable
Relevant
Timely

So, instead of "Lose Weight," set a goal to "Walk 10,000 steps a day and limit your caloric intake to 2,000 calories a day." If that's too overwhelming, start with one and then add in the other once you're comfortable in your new routine.

Instead of "Save Money," set a goal to save 15% of each paycheck and reduce expenses by 10%.

Instead of "Change Careers," set a goal to update your resume, sign up for job alerts, and network with 4 to 5 people each month.

One year I wanted to focus on fitness but I was very overwhelmed, facing what felt like a huge commitment to exercise. So I started by dedicating at least 5 minutes every day to fitness. I wrote down "Five 4 Fit" on an index card and hung it up on my bathroom mirror to serve as a daily reminder of my goal. I am happy to say that by starting out small, I was able to commit to my goal by exercising daily as part of my routine.

> **TRY THIS**
>
> If you were to set one resolution for the coming year, what would it be? How can you turn that into a SMART goal? Are you up for the challenge? How will you track your progress and reward yourself along the way?

> **READ MORE**
>
> The Lingering Task
> The "Someday" List
> Bringing Your Vision to Life

38

BRINGING YOUR VISION TO LIFE

Once you've set a dream or vision for yourself, what next?

The biggest reasons for failing to realize our resolution are having too many goals, setting unrealistic goals, not keeping track of progress, and forgetting about the goal, or losing interest. However, if you are truly committed to making a change, none of these obstacles can stand in your way.

Setting the goal is the starting point, and for many, it's often the ending point as well. You may have selected a goal, but you get busy, people demand your attention, you get distracted by other things, and before you know it, several months have passed by without much progress. Sound familiar?

It doesn't have to end at the beginning. Once you've identified your theme of the year, devote some time to thinking about the specific things you will do to achieve that goal or make change. Write down distinct, measurable tasks that can be done in a set amount of time. Then, take that list and prioritize it. Start by selecting the top three first, knowing that you can always go back and pick a few more.

Just as important as completing tasks, is documenting your progress. One easy and reliable way to track your progress is by keeping up with your "done" list that we introduced earlier. It will feel good to write down what you've done and it's a great motivator to visually see all that you have accomplished. Also, hopefully you'll start seeing real-world benefits as well.

To stay focused over time, creating a vision board can inspire you and reinforce your commitment to your goals. Set aside some time to gather images, photos, quotes, headlines, and other materials and use them to create a collage to hang in your office or bedroom. This visual representation of your goals and desires serves as a powerful reminder and subconscious motivator each time you see it.

I currently have two vision boards – one for my professional aspirations and one for my more personal ones. I prefer to do them the old fashioned way with lots of magazines and cork boards but in this digital age, there are a lot of online options as well. If you use Canva, they have hundreds of vision board templates you can use for free and upload your own photos, images, and quotes.

TRY THIS

What's your personal theme for the coming year? What are some specific tasks that you can do to achieve your goal? What would you put on a vision board to help you visualize your goal and motivate you to achieve it?

READ MORE

The Perfect To-Do List is a Prioritized One
The "Done" List
Creating New Habits

THE PRIORITIZATION PUZZLE

Earlier in the book we recognized that prioritizing your tasks is a critical success factor for increasing your productivity. And, we also acknowledged that prioritization is more challenging than it sounds. Some days, it feels like everything is a priority. At other times, it's not clear what should come first. Many times, we just prioritize what's the easiest and simplest to get done or the things we enjoy doing.

Even if we wanted to prioritize our tasks, where do we begin and how do we make intelligent decisions about what to tackle first and what can wait? The good news is that smarter people who came before us figured out a system that we can use to help us out.

The key to unlocking the mystery of prioritization originated from an unlikely source, President Dwight D. Eisenhower. In a speech, he quoted the President of Northwestern University who explained, "I have two kinds of problems: the urgent and the important. The urgent are not important, and the important are never urgent."

Some years later, in his book, *The 7 Habits of Highly Effective People*, renowned author Stephen Covey took what became known as the Eisenhower Principle and developed it further to create the Eisenhower Matrix or the Time Management Matrix.[21] This is what my version of the matrix looks like:

	URGENT	NOT URGENT
IMPORTANT	DO IT	SCHEDULE IT
NOT IMPORTANT	DELEGATE IT OR DELAY IT	DELETE IT

Having an objective and clear understanding of these categories is critical to making this matrix work for me.

As things come my way, I first determine the level of urgency and importance of each task. Urgent tasks need immediate attention and would have direct consequences if ignored. Important tasks are more strategic and significantly impact my ability to achieve my goals. Once I have labeled my tasks with both indicators, I can then determine the best order in which to tackle them.

URGENT AND IMPORTANT: JUST DO IT

The most obvious priorities are those that are both urgent and important. These should be at the top of your list and should become one of your "Daily Top Three" tasks. These are the types of things you want to address right away and reap the benefits.

NOT URGENT, BUT IMPORTANT: SCHEDULE IT

These tasks often get lost in the mix. While you know they are important, they tend to take the back seat to urgent items. You think you'll get to these important tasks eventually, but eventually never arrives. Block time on your calendar to focus on these tasks to complete them.

URGENT, BUT NOT IMPORTANT: DELEGATE OR DELAY

Even if something seems urgent, if it's not important, don't prioritize it. Question whether the task should belong to you. The Eisenhower Matrix guides you to delegate these tasks, but if you don't have someone you can ask for help, delay doing it. I often find that sometimes these tasks go away on their own when they are no longer seemingly urgent.

NOT URGENT OR IMPORTANT: DELETE IT

Ignore, delete, and move on. Many of us take on tasks, even prioritizing them, because they seem like a quick win. However, these menial assignments take time away from impactful tasks. If you can get used to identifying the tasks that fall into this category, you will save yourself a lot of time and effort.

TRY THIS

Take your to do list and categorize your tasks according to urgency and importance. Take those that are urgent and important and prioritize them. Delete those that are neither. For those tasks that remain, schedule time on your calendar to focus on the most important ones and delay others for the time being.

READ MORE

The Perfect To-Do List is a Prioritized One
Cultivating Your Lists
The Two-Minute Rule

THE JUGGLING ACT

No matter how much we try to manage our tasks and our time, we inevitably end up having more to do than is humanly possible. Most of us can relate to this imbalance as a never-ending juggling act as we try to keep all of the balls off the floor. We're all just trying not to drop the ball.

In real life, no matter how good we are at juggling the many tasks on our plate, inevitably some balls will drop. We must accept that this is just part of the game and not a game ender. More importantly, the more we understand the balls we are juggling, the better we become at playing the game.

Pretend there are three balls in the game of life: glass, plastic, and rubber balls. Success is understanding which category the things you are juggling fall into. Sometimes, identifying the categories of the balls can be more challenging than the act of juggling itself.

GLASS BALLS

Glass balls will shatter if they fall. These are the things that need your immediate and focused attention. They are the things that are most important, cannot be delayed or delegated, and will have negative consequences if dropped.

A few years ago, my father's health started deteriorating and we weren't sure what his recovery would look like. While I would try to visit him in Virginia as often as possible, it wasn't nearly enough. I immediately made it a top priority to visit him every three weeks or so to maximize our time together and provide the support my family needed. For me, this glass ball rose to the top of my priorities and took precedence over many other things that until then had seemingly been important.

PLASTIC BALLS

These balls will fall but will not break. They may crack, but they won't break. They will lay on the ground and roll around until they can be picked back up again. These tasks don't require immediate attention and can be picked back up later as time allows.

Most parents of young children know the importance of reading to their children as aiding in cognitive development, fostering a love of learning, and creating memories of quality time spent together. When my kids were young, I tried really hard to spend time reading together every night.

While well-intentioned, that goal wasn't realistic. Some nights my kids were cranky or I was tired and some days there just wasn't enough time. This became a ball that I could let drop and pick up on the days it made sense. Neither one of my adult children have complained that we didn't read enough together.

RUBBER BALLS

When dropped, rubber balls continue to bounce around by themselves for a while. There's no immediate or negative impact from letting rubber balls drop every now and then. They can easily be picked back up when you have the bandwidth.

Do you know the recommended timelines for cleaning your bathroom? Apparently, the CDC and EPA have developed generally accepted hygiene practices. We're supposed to wipe down the counters and dry the shower walls and doors daily! We should clean the toilet, scrub the shower, and mop the bathroom floors every week. And, do a full, deep cleaning every month.

For me, this is clearly a rubber ball I get to when I can, and honestly, I think it's OK to let this chore bounce around for a while.

That said, do keep in mind that the rubber balls will eventually run out of inertia and stop bouncing if left alone for too long. I can almost guarantee that if you put it off for too long, you can expect some negative consequences. I experienced this nightmare first-hand when I went to visit my son's apartment during his first year at college – you really don't want to see what happens when you never clean your bathroom!

To recap, a successful juggling act dictates that you never drop a glass ball. Glass balls should command all of your focus and attention. If you need to drop a ball, try to drop a rubber ball you can pick back up later. And, if you drop a plastic ball, it'll be OK, no permanent damage will be done… unless you continually drop the same plastic ball.

TRY THIS

How many balls are you juggling right now? Can you categorize them into glass, plastic, and rubber balls? What can you do to make sure you don't drop any glass balls? If necessary, which rubber balls can you let go for now?

READ MORE

The Fallacy of Doing it All
One Balanced Life to Live
Managing Your Energy

BIG ROCKS AND LITTLE ROCKS

We all struggle with prioritizing the big things in life and making the time and finding the focus to tackle them – especially when it's so easy to knock out the little things that give us instant gratification. When I was working at The Weather Channel, I printed out the graphic below and hung it in my office.

What are you spending your time on?

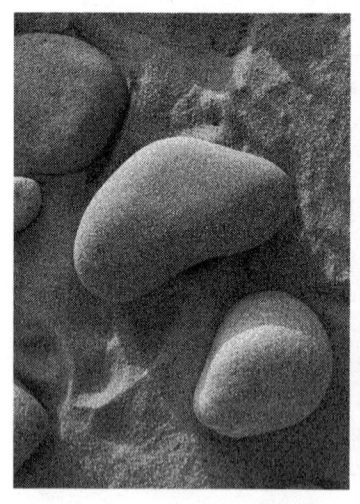

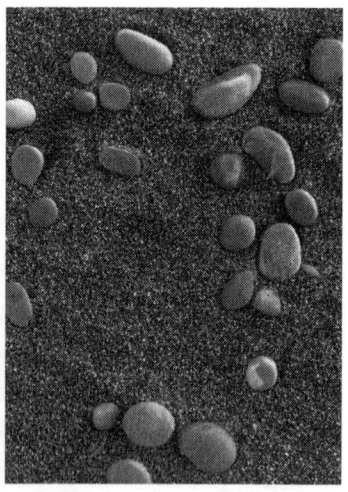

It often caught people's attention, serving as a substantive conversation starter about their work, priorities, time management, and how they could focus more of their energy on the big rocks versus the little rocks.

When faced with a daunting list of tasks, most of us would tackle the quick and easy ones first. And, why not?

A few small wins can make you feel good in the short term, but is this the right approach for the long term? You might recall the visual demonstration of life's bucket by Stephen Covey. If you fill your bucket first with sand, then gravel, you will run out of space for the bigger rocks. However, if you start with big rocks first, followed by gravel, and finally sand, the smaller items will settle into the gaps between the bigger ones.[22]

This makes sense in the physical world, but how do we apply this to real life? How do we make sure we are putting the big rocks first, when it's so easy to get side-tracked by the gravel and sand? Nowadays, it's more difficult than ever with constant dings and pings clamoring for our attention.

Think of sending emails and texts as sand. Attending meetings are small rocks and your projects and deliverables are big rocks. If you prioritize emails and texts they will easily fill up your day. Same with meetings. And, at the end of the day, I bet, you won't have made any progress on your big rocks!

Start by prioritizing your MITs, or the "big rocks," for each day. You don't have to prioritize the little things, they will just naturally fall into place. You don't need to put "eat lunch" or "check email" or "go to the bathroom" on your list of priorities because you will naturally make the time to take care of those things. It's the big, important, and hard things you need to identify and find dedicated time to focus on getting done.

TRY THIS

What are you spending your time on? What are the big rocks that you need or want to tackle? How much time are you currently dedicating to the big rocks versus the little rocks? How can you adjust your schedule or your priorities to make time for those big rocks?

READ MORE

The Most Important Tasks
One Balanced Life to Live
The Prioritization Puzzle

THE THREE LIST ASSESSMENT

Each fall, the leaves start changing colors. Football is being played across the country. Signs of the upcoming holiday season are popping up everywhere and you suddenly realize there are only a few weeks left in the year. It's the perfect time to assess the progress you've made against your personal and professional resolutions.

What did you set out to do this year? How are you faring against those goals? Do you even remember what they were? At the end of the year, many employers ask you to assess your own performance as an input to year-end reviews which may impact bonuses or salary increases. Take the time to see how you've done so far and what you can do over the next few months to make sure you hit all of your targets.

First, figure out where you stand against your goals. Then, use this easy exercise to make any needed adjustments: identify the top three things you should "stop," "start," or "continue" doing. Periodically, I use this three list methodology to assess progress against a deliverable, project, or personal goal.

STOP

Which activities take up a lot of your time but are not helping you achieve your goals? Consider time spent in meetings, writing reports, responding to emails, or with a particularly needy colleague. You will quickly realize many of these things can be eliminated, delayed, or delegated. Pick three you can stop doing without impacting your goals.

START

With your newly found time, think about three things you can start doing that will help you achieve your goals. For example, did you resolve to exercise more? Try skipping one meeting each week and getting outside for a walk during that time. Instead of responding to every email, is there some more valuable work you can focus on instead? Come up with three specific tasks that will get you closer to achieving your goals and prioritize them for the next few months.

CONTINUE

What have you been doing that has brought you closer to achieving your goals? Identify three productive activities and keep doing them. Being aware of these will help you to continue to prioritize these activities. You may even think of ways to increase or improve these tasks.

You can also use this methodology with work groups. Ask your colleagues to make a list of things to stop, start, or continue around particular topics. You may just find that everyone is on the same page.

TRY THIS

What progress have you made in achieving your resolutions or goals? If you've been keeping a "done" list, this will be easy to assess. Once you understand the gap and know what is left to do, schedule an hour this week to create your "stop," "start," and "continue" items. Once you've created these lists, adjust your calendar to eliminate those things you are going to "stop" and schedule in the ones you are going to "start."

READ MORE

Less is More
The Most Important Tasks
One Balanced Life to Live

43

THE RULE OF THREE

Many things in life come in threes. It's not a coincidence – there's truly an art and science behind using the rule of three. This principle suggests that things that come in threes are more interesting, enjoyable, and memorable and offer a certain balance and rhythm.

In fact, the Latin phrase "omne trium perfectum" loosely translates to everything that comes in threes is perfect. Here are some of my favorite examples:

first, second, third
past, present, future
red, white, and blue
hot, warm, cold
beginning, middle, end
small, medium, large
sun, sea, and sand
ABC, 123, XYZ
red, yellow, green
yesterday, today, tomorrow
stop, drop, roll
life, liberty, and the pursuit of happiness
big, bigger, biggest
high, medium, low
conceive, believe, achieve
stop, look, listen
gold, silver, bronze
earth, wind, fire
knife, fork, spoon
vanilla, chocolate, strawberry
stop, start, continue

When I started putting together my own prioritization system, I came up with the concept of the "Daily Top Three" in alignment with this principle. Each day, before tackling anything, I think about my goals, review my task list and select my top three tasks for the day. Not one, not two or four or five – just three!

Just as the rule suggests, having three tasks is easy to remember, appears manageable, and offers the right amount of challenge. There are days that I can get more than three tasks done and other days, I barely manage to get through one. But, at the end of the day, no matter how many tasks I complete, I still select three more tasks to focus on the next day. It just feels right.

> **TRY THIS**
>
> What are some of your favorite sequences of three I might have missed?
>
> Take a look at your to-do list and pick three tasks to focus on and get them done. Once those three are complete, pick three more.

> **READ MORE**
>
> The Most Important Tasks

GETTING OVER FEELING OVERWHELMED

When life gets particularly busy, it's easy to get overwhelmed by it all. Most of us push through the rough patch hoping things will eventually calm down. But in my experience, it takes a great strategy to get to the other side.

In most cases, rejuvenating activities like getting a good night's sleep, exercising, or going out for a delicious meal help us reset our energy levels. However, when this "out of control" feeling persists, impacting our physical health, mental wellbeing, and stress levels, we tend not to prioritize self-care activities over everything else.

In the past, when I would feel overwhelmed, I would take it hour by hour, one step at a time. I thought if I trudged on, things would eventually get better. They never did. Just keeping up with it all was not a good long-term solution.

I remember one particularly busy period when my kids had a lot going on, which meant I also had a lot on my plate, and my daughter got an invitation to spend the night at a friend's house. I told her that we can't always do everything we want to which she responded, "Can't you just work it out?"

Ideally, I should be able to delete, delegate, or delay some tasks, but that's not always an option. When your plate is overflowing, here are some quick and easy things you can use to help you get through without losing your sanity.

PUT IT ON PAPER

It doesn't matter where or how, but write down how you're feeling. Writing things down gets it out of your head, allowing you to feel more calm and less cluttered. Typically, this can be done in just a few minutes.

CALL A FRIEND

Sharing how you're feeling with a friend will help you feel less alone and connecting with others will help you recharge your batteries. We often feel alone when times get tough, but more often than not, what you're experiencing is not unique to you. Grab lunch or coffee or go on a walk together to double the value of the time spent.

GET PHYSICAL

There are activities you can do to relieve the physical symptoms of stress and anxiety. Do an intense workout, pull weeds from the garden, scream out loud, or do a deep cleaning. Have you heard of rage rooms? I'm not recommending these, but there are places you can go to safely break and destroy things to relieve your stress. For some, the act of smashing things can help release pent-up emotions.

Test out different tactics to find which work best for you. The next time you're feeling overwhelmed you'll find taking 10 to 15 minutes to try one of the aforementioned activities will be well worth the short investment of time.

> **TRY THIS**
>
> Instead of muscling through it, take a timeout. Carve out a small window of time to write, connect with a friend, or get physical. It won't reduce the number of things on your to-do list, but it will help how you're feeling about it all.

> **READ MORE**
>
> The Fallacy of Doing it All
> One Balanced Life to Live
> Managing Your Energy

MANAGING YOUR ENERGY

We've discovered there are things we control and others that we have an illusion of managing. The one area we have full control over, but don't pay much attention to, is how we use our energy. In every case, we decide how to spend our time and the level of energy we're willing to expend to get those tasks done.

Think about the energy you put into walking versus jogging versus running. At the heart of the activity, you're moving from one point to another, but the amount of energy required is variable. We walk to grab the mail or take the dog out, but if we're participating in a neighborhood 5K, we run. We choose to utilize the right amount of energy for the task at hand.

What if we apply this same filter to other areas of our lives? How much of our energy do we devote to the things that really matter? How much of our energy gets wasted on activities that are time-consuming and arduous, yet unproductive?

I used to think I had to give 110% to every activity. Watering the plants, writing a report, making dinner, or planning a party. After all, the more energy you give, the better the outcome, right? Not always. No matter how energetically you do certain activities, the output isn't necessarily improved. I had to learn that I don't have to run to everything; sometimes walking is sufficient.

Look at this another way. What happens when you put all your energy into a workout versus just doing the movements? How does an audience respond when you put energy into a presentation instead of just reading from a script? Think about the difference it makes when you study hard for an exam and when you just show up unprepared.

How you use your energy matters, but don't overlook recharging your battery. Recovery activities, including sleep, relaxation, meditation, or whatever else refills your tank, are all critical to maintaining elevated energy levels.

On the other side of the coin are things that deplete your energy, worrying being the number one example. Worrying puts an enormous strain on us both physically and emotionally and leaves us drained without leading us anywhere. Needlessly fretting over outcomes we can't control leaves us no better off.

Overthinking can have the same effect of sucking your energy. Do you find yourself going round and round in circles only to find yourself back in the same place you began? Not only are you not moving yourself forward, but the process itself is dizzying.

When you find yourself needlessly worrying or overthinking, try to find ways to redirect that energy into activities with more positive and productive outcomes.

TRY THIS

How have you spent your energy over the past few days? Was it focused on the most important things? What tasks did you find you had no energy left for? What could you have done differently? Did you prioritize your recovery activities?

READ MORE

The Myth of Time Management
The Fallacy of Doing it All
One Balanced Life to Live

46

ALWAYS HAVE A PLAN "B"

No big surprise, I am a firm believer in planning your work and working your plan. But I am also a realist, recognizing that the best-laid plans don't always pan out and seemingly there's nothing we can do about it. Or, is there?

We should always have a backup plan.

Sadly, my dear father lost his parents and many family members at a very young age during the partition of India in 1947. As Hindus living in what is now Pakistan, they had to flee their homes and leave everything behind to resettle in India. During one of the largest global mass migrations, many violent riots broke out between the Muslims and the Hindus which resulted in the deaths of approximately a million people.

I don't exactly remember exactly when I learned about my family history, but it has been with me my entire life. From a very early age I often pondered and "planned" what I would do if I were caught in a similar situation. For many years, I wore a gold necklace that I would never remove because I planned to sell or negotiate with it should the need arise. And still to this day, I think about what I would take with me if I were forced to leave my home.

History and lived experience was the impetus for me to think about having a backup plan. Today, I always have a "Plan B" for all things big or small over a spectrum of "what if" situations.

For example, if I get a flat tire, I will call AAA. If I don't get invited to the party, I'll call another friend to go to dinner with me. If I fail my exam, I will talk to my professor. If I don't get the raise I was expecting, I'll share my list of accomplishments (my "Done" list) with my boss to demonstrate my value.

Your turn: If you _____, you will _____.

When you go through this exercise enough you will realize that your options are endless as long as you're open to recognizing and embracing them. Having a backup plan is not planning for failure. In fact, it's planning for success no matter the roadblocks.

Here are some of the reasons why it's always beneficial to have an alternative plan.

REDUCES YOUR ANXIETY

If you have a backup plan, there's less pressure on you to make sure the default plan succeeds without a hitch. If you know there's a fallback option, you can let your plan play out knowing that you're prepared if it gets derailed.

YOU HAVE OPTIONS

Making a contingency plan reminds you that there's not just one path to reaching your goal. There may be a more direct path, but if you have to take a scenic route to get to the same destination, that's OK too. So, there's no harm in planning several different ways to get to your goal ahead of needing it.

YOU'RE EMPOWERED

Having a backup plan gives you more control over the situation. You are not just waiting for things to happen for you. You have more influence if you have multiple ways forward to help you get to your end goal. And, if and when things don't go according to your plan, you don't have to panic and wonder what to do next.

> **TRY THIS**
>
> What's one of the big rocks that you're thinking about or working on right now? Do you have a contingency plan? If not, what could that be? How can you hedge your bets to make sure you have a backup plan to achieve your goals?

> **READ MORE**
>
> It's All About Time Blocking
> Double or Nothing
> Go With the Flow

THE VALUE OF BEING ORGANIZED

Over the years, many of my friends and colleagues have commented on my organizational abilities. I take great pride in this compliment since I work very hard at being organized. I religiously follow the Two-Minute Rule. I always make sure things are put back in their place. I live by my lists to the point that everyone knows (and even jokes) about them.

However, at times I wonder if this obsession of mine is worthwhile. Does the time and energy spent on becoming organized help my productivity or would it be better spent on getting stuff done? Naturally, I did some research and some soul-searching to dig deeper.

One definition of "organized" is: "having one's affairs in order so as to deal with them efficiently," implying an inherent benefit. Second, a 2008 study conducted by the National Association of Professional Organizers revealed that, "27% of respondents feel disorganized at work, and of those, 91% said they would be more effective and efficient if they were more organized."[23] Third, when I searched for the plus sides of being organized, hundreds of articles popped up listing the countless benefits from health, to efficiency, to style and brand, and even to your reputation.

And, in the words of the very wise Benjamin Franklin:

"For every minute spent organizing, an hour is earned."

Now, that sounds very valuable to me! So, with all that said, here are the measurable benefits reaped from the time and energy spent staying organized.

SAVES TIME

Because I have a home for everything and I put everything back in its place, I never waste time looking for anything. I also schedule my full day so I don't wonder what I need to do next. I start with my meetings and appointments and then fill in the top priority tasks for the day to make sure I have allocated time to get them done. Very little of my time is time wasted.

INCREASES RELIABILITY

Thanks to my to-do list, I very rarely forget things that need to be done. I know that my brain isn't good for remembering things so I make sure I always write down my tasks. Because I block time on my calendar to complete tasks and to focus on deep work, I never miss a deadline. This combination of my to-do list and my calendar management ensures that I meet my commitments and deliver on expectations.

REDUCES MY STRESS

By maintaining a clean house, I don't have to rush to clean before having guests over. I don't stress about where things are or what needs to get done. I don't worry about what I might be forgetting or leaving things to the last minute. Because I have a plan in place, when urgent issues arise, as they often do, I can easily adjust and reset expectations as needed.

> **TRY THIS**
>
> Think about how organized or unorganized you are. Identify a specific area of your life that feels chaotic. Is there a simple system you could make routine to become more organized? What is the value in becoming more organized in that specific area? Is that benefit enough to warrant spending the time being proactive?

> **READ MORE**
>
> The Magic of a Single To-Do List
> A Place for Everything
> Productivity Requires Perseverance

YOUR EFFECTIVENESS

---

*Efficiency is doing things right;
effectiveness is doing the right things.*

Peter F. Drucker

YOUR EFFECTIVENESS

No doubt, we've been through a lot together (some might say we've been very *productive!*), but, the best is yet to come. So far, we've covered ways to optimize your time, manage your lists, make the most of your day, and maximize your life. And while all of these suggestions will help you become more efficient and productive, the ideas we'll cover in the following chapters can be truly transformational by helping you put these concepts to work for you.

If you think you've read enough, or if you're not ready to roll up your sleeves and get your hands dirty, you might consider stopping here. When I wrote this book, I quickly realized that it wasn't necessarily meant to be read in any specific order or from beginning to end. In fact, I wanted to make sure you could easily pick it back up at any given point in time to find whatever it is you're looking for that may be relevant at that moment. Honestly, implementing even just a few of these strategies will dramatically improve your productivity.

So if you need to focus on what you've learned so far and then come back to this section when you're ready for more, feel free. As you know by now, I believe that it's better to make slow and steady progress, rather than trying to tackle everything at once.

I'm hoping you've learned what you need to do to be more productive and when to do it, but now you'll see the way you approach productivity can be life changing.

In the coming chapters, we'll dig deeper into what it really takes to be hyper-productive. We'll examine characteristics of productive people, the value of purpose, and the pitfalls and distractions that can get in the way.

We'll also address the importance of following up, being resourceful and disciplined, and creating new habits. Without developing and honing these skills, increasing your efficiency and effectiveness will continue to be a challenge.

These last few chapters cover the areas I struggle with the most. Honestly, I wrote them so I can re-read them as a reminder that in order to be fully productive, I have to set boundaries, ask for help, and embrace feedback.

48

PRODUCTIVITY REQUIRES PERSEVERANCE

What makes some people more productive than others? Are some people born organized and productive? Or, is this a skill we can learn and develop over time? And, why does it seemingly come naturally to some while others struggle?

No matter where you're starting from, improving your productivity requires perseverance and resilience. It doesn't just show up on a silver platter one day, and it's certainly not for the faint of heart. Each one of these tactics requires focus, practice, and tenacity. After all, you're training your mind to think differently and you have to shift your mindset which won't miraculously change overnight.

In her book, *Grit: The Power of Passion and Perseverance*, Angela Duckworth interviewed a wide range of successful people to uncover what they all had in common. Surprisingly, it wasn't talent, education, or even IQ. She found that the key to their success was a combination of passion and perseverance which she labeled *grit*.[24] Successful people find their purpose and then fight tooth and nail.

Good news is, we aren't doomed if we weren't born knowing the laws of productivity. For me, this was the biggest motivator to figuring it out. I knew there had to be a smarter way to approach managing it all.

I enthusiastically took on the challenge – one step at a time.

My fighting spirit first surfaced long ago. My family immigrated to the United States from England when I was ten years old. As an Indian girl with a British accent, I looked and sounded different. I quickly became a curiosity amongst the other fifth graders at my elementary school, and not in a good way. Even earlier, in England, kids on the playground would point fingers at me and yell out, "Blackie Paki." I wanted to run home and hide under the covers forever. But something inside me kept me going.

These defining moments made me realize my innate drive to fight and overcome. I wasn't going to let these kids make me feel badly or stop me from moving forward. Once I had made that decision, it was much easier for me to ignore them. Once I uncovered the strength to get past their taunting, I then realized I could do the same for other obstacles or challenges I would face. From that moment on, I truly believed I could do whatever I set my mind to. The fire was lit, and each challenge brought more fuel.

Over the years, choosing fight over flight has helped me develop and hone so many of the skills I've shared with you.

Can you recall a time that you were faced with a particularly challenging situation? How did you handle a tough situation at work, an emotionally difficult breakup, or an unforeseen health condition? Adversity is a given when you take on any new challenge, however, the most successful people are the ones who learn how to navigate them.

> **TRY THIS**
>
> Like so many of the suggestions in this book, grit can be learned, developed, and honed. In fact, a good way to get started is to pick one of the recommendations in this book and stay the course until it sticks. Once you get going, there's no stopping you!

> **READ MORE**
>
> Cultivating Your Lists
> The Value of Being Organized
> Creating New Habits

THE IMPORTANCE OF WHY

In his highly acclaimed productivity book *Smarter, Better, Faster*, Charles Duhigg opens with a chapter about motivation. He asserts that those who have control and understand the big picture are more motivated. He writes, "If you can link something hard to a choice you care about, it makes the task easier." He adds, "Make a chore into a meaningful decision, and self-motivation will emerge."[25]

So many of us spend a lot of time and energy making lists, tracking tasks, and keeping up with all the things that we need to get done. But, how many of us are asking, "Why?"

- Why should I do this task?
- Why is this task important?
- Why should I spend any time on this task?
- Why is this beneficial?

Early in my career, someone shared a great story that stuck with me and I have since shared this anecdote with many of my colleagues over the years. A man is walking by a construction site and comes across three workers doing the same job. He stops and asks the first one, "What are you doing?" The man replies, "I am laying bricks." He then asks the second guy the same question to which he responds, "I am building a wall." The man then turns to the third guy and asks the same question, but this time, the worker stands, pauses and smiles, and looking to the sky affirms, "I am constructing a cathedral."Through their descriptions of their work, you can probably tell which of the three workers would be most motivated, driven, and productive.

At the time I was a Marketing Coordinator, trying to understand the purpose of my work. I attempted to map out how my tasks and accomplishments impacted (even slightly) my team's and the company's overall goals. Also, I thought about what we were trying to accomplish in the big picture and volunteered to help out in areas that could be more impactful. During quarterly investor calls, I would get excited to hear our results believing that I had contributed to achieving those goals.

Next time you're about to start a new task, begin by asking yourself, "Why?" If you can't come up with a strong answer, maybe consider removing that task from your list and move on to the things that have greater meaning and significance. You will find that working on the things you really care about is enough to motivate you to complete them.

TRY THIS

Think about those tasks you find joy in doing. What motivates you to do them? What drives you to get them done? Then, think about some of the things that linger on your list. Why don't they get done? Think about how you can attach a greater meaning to those tasks to increase your motivation to tackle them. If you're struggling to find meaning, are they really that important?

READ MORE

Making the Most of Your Time
The Most Important Tasks
Make SMARTer Resolutions

FIVE PRODUCTIVITY PITFALLS

At the start of something new, whether it be a new year, new job, or new project, we often begin bright-eyed and bushy-tailed with all the good intentions in the world. So what happens? Somewhere along the way, we are derailed and may find ourselves distracted and without clear direction.

Here are five pitfalls that can directly impact your productivity. Learn to become aware of them so you can steer clear of these stumbling blocks.

DIGITAL DISTRACTIONS

The number one deterrent to your productivity is the amount of time you spend checking your email and browsing social media or playing games. Turn off all notifications and schedule time for these digital distractions as your reward for completing a very important task or project. In *Deep Work: Rules for Focused Success in a Distracted World*, Cal Newport shares strategies to help you avoid distractions and stay focused in order to produce innovative and meaningful output.

MEETINGS

According to Flowtrace's *50 Surprising Meeting Statistics for 2024*, we spend 33 to 50% of our working time in meetings and most of them are a total waste of time. Before blindly accepting meeting invites, think critically about whether attending the meeting is a good use of your time. If you must attend or hold a meeting, make the most of the time by following the guidelines in the chapter, "Making Meetings Work Again" for conducting effective meetings. Also, Patrick Lencioni's book, *Death by Meeting*, is another great resource.

PROCRASTINATING

Everyone's got that one task they're putting off. Consider why you are avoiding it. Is it not that important? Is it too daunting? Or, are you unmotivated? Understanding the importance of why you should do the task will help you find the motivation to attack the task head on. Check out more tips in the chapter on "The Constraints of Procrastination"

MULTITASKING

This is my biggest weakness. When we have too much to do we just keep trying to do it all and sometimes all at once. However, science has proven that it's technically impossible for us to truly multitask and the costs of constantly switching between tasks has such an impact that it's just not worth doing. Instead, schedule focused time to work on the most important things you need to get done. For more on this, see my chapter "To Multitask or Not to Multitask."

YOUR PHONE

According to a 2023 survey by Reviews.org, average Americans check their phones 144 times per day and spend an average of 4 hours and 25 minutes each day on their phones![26] Stop letting your phone negatively control your time and start using it to increase your productivity.

When you need to focus, try putting your phone in a drawer or in another room. You may be reluctant to do this, but try it and see what happens.

> **TRY THIS**
>
> What are the pitfalls that impact your productivity? What are three things you can do to eliminate or avoid those pitfalls? How can you hold yourself accountable to steering clear of those pitfalls?

> **READ MORE**
>
> The Constraints of Procrastination
> To Multitask or Not to Multitask?
> Making Meetings Work Again

THE BIGGEST PRODUCTIVITY PROBLEM

There's a single thing that has the biggest negative impact on our productivity every day. We all do it. We are all guilty of it no matter how good our intentions. So, what is it?

Not following through or following up on our commitments.

It's so easy to say, "I'll call you tomorrow." Or, "Let's meet for lunch." Sometimes we say, "I'll send you that article as soon as I get back to my desk." Or, "I'll have that report done by the end of the week." These promises set an expectation that the recipient believes to be true, however, all of us are guilty at one time or another of dropping the ball on the follow through.

So, why don't we follow through on the commitments we make?

WE SIMPLY FORGET WHAT WE SAID

Our brains are full, our bodies are active, and our days are busy, and sometimes these seemingly small promises fall by the wayside. A surefire way to ensure that you follow up is to write it down. As soon as you make a commitment, no matter how big or small, add it to your to-do list. That way it'll serve as a reminder whenever you check your lists.

WE DON'T REALLY MEAN IT

Too often we say without giving weight to our words. Some of my favorites are:

"See you tomorrow." (Well, will you really?)
"Let's get together." (Then, set a date and time.)
"I'll be right there." (Like, now or in 30 minutes?)
"I'm almost done." (Again, tell me how much longer.)

WE OVERESTIMATE OUR ABILITY TO DELIVER

Most of the time, we have good intentions but are unable to keep a commitment for one reason or another. Maybe that report took longer than expected because something came up preventing you from finishing. As soon as you know you aren't going to be able to meet a commitment, let that person know and re-establish expectations. Don't wait for the other person to reach out to you to find out what's going on.

TRY THIS

Next time you commit to something, stop, write it down, and then come up with a plan to make sure you can meet that expectation. If someone has to follow up with you on a commitment you made, think through how it got dropped and determine how you can close that communication gap the next time. Before they reach out, think about recent commitments you may have made and whether you can deliver on your promises.

READ MORE

The Magic of a Single To-Do List
The Two-Minute Rule
How Being Busy Breeds Productivity

THE THREE R'S OF PRODUCTIVITY

The often misunderstood key to increasing productivity is to do fewer things. We can focus on doing the most important things well when we aren't trying to do everything all at once.

Reference the three R's of productivity to identify and eliminate the distractions that eat up your time and energy.

REDUCE

You don't have to do everything that's on your to-do list. As outlined in the chapter "Prioritize the Perfect To-Do List," it's a good idea to get in the habit of reviewing your list daily to prioritize the most important tasks and determine if there are things on your list that aren't important or no longer need attention.

Keep in mind that it's OK to remove items from your list. If they truly are important, they will come back around. If there's a task that's been lingering on your list for over two weeks, that's a sign that perhaps it really isn't that important and can be removed.

REUSE

Before you begin a task, see if there's something you have already created that you can leverage. For example, a proposal or press release that you've already written can often be repurposed. Also, before you create a new document or presentation, look for templates to help you get started. Microsoft and Google have large libraries of templates available for their products.

And, with convenient access to AI tools there's a wealth of information right at your fingertips. You may be surprised how many free resources are available online! Don't reinvent the wheel if the heavy lifting has already been done for you.

REASSIGN

Just because you can get something done, doesn't mean that you should always be the one to do it. Think critically about the tasks that can be handled by someone else. It may feel easier to just do it yourself, but think about the opportunity cost of what doesn't get done during that time. Could your time be better spent? Keep John C. Maxwell's advice in mind:

> "If something can be done 80% as well by someone else, delegate."

TRY THIS

Look at your to-do list. Which things on your list don't need to be done? Think about which items can be removed or reassigned. See what already exists that you can leverage that might reduce the amount of time you need to spend on it.

As we have learned, cleansing, and curating your list is just as important as creating one.

READ MORE

Prioritize the Perfect To-Do List
Cultivating Your Lists
Less is More
The Prioritization Puzzle

HOW BEING BUSY BREEDS PRODUCTIVITY

Why does it seem that the busiest people get the most done? It's certainly not just because they are busy. As we discovered in the chapter about maximizing your time, being busy and being productive are two very different things. You can be busy with distractions and time-sucks and you can also be productive solving a difficult problem while on a walk. But, while they are very different, busyness and productivity can work hand in hand.

I'm sure you have heard Benjamin Franklin's famous quote:

> "If you want something done, ask a busy person."

I have often wondered why this was the case. Logically, it would seem that people who aren't as busy would have the most time and ability to get a task done.

While working in the corporate world, juggling work, home, and two student athletes, I was often the one asked to take on more, and for the most part I did. Interestingly, when I was running my own business and was soon-to-be an empty nester, I found myself less productive. My to-do list kept growing and tasks lingered for much longer.

I am living proof that the busiest people are indeed the most productive. Here are a few reasons why busy people get more done.

THEY HAVE A SYSTEM

Busy people must be organized to keep up with everything they need to do. They routinely use systems to support them like calendars, to-do lists, notes, and communication tools. They have a process and are disciplined in sticking to it. They have a place and priority for everything.

THEY ARE RELIABLE

Busy people deliver on their commitments. They agree to do something and get it done and then in turn, they are asked to take on more because they are dependable. The more they do successfully, the more they are asked to do, a potentially vicious cycle.

The biggest struggle for busy people is learning to say "No" to tasks that are unimportant or can be delegated to someone else. More on that to come.

THEY DON'T PROCRASTINATE

Busy people don't have a lot of free time. As such, they must prepare for the unexpected. When a new task comes up, busy people try to tackle it as quickly as possible. To make sure it gets done, they will schedule time, and often a backup time to ensure they can follow through. Recurring tasks for busy people are routinely scheduled to protect the time on their calendars.

At the other extreme, people with a lot of free time tend to kick tasks down the road resulting in those pesky lingering tasks.

THEY ARE FOCUSED

Because there's so much to do, busy people recognize the importance of full focus. They know they need to complete their task at hand as efficiently as possible to move on to the next thing on their list. They do not have the luxury of dilly-dallying.

TRY THIS

How busy are you? Look at your busier days and compare them to some of your not-so-busy days. Do you notice a difference in the level of your productivity?

READ MORE

The Constraints of Procrastination
A Perfectly Productive Day
Productivity Requires Perseverance

54

DON'T BREAK THE CHAIN

Comedian Jerry Seinfeld popularized one of the most important productivity and habit-forming techniques when he stated and restated, "Don't break the chain!" He claimed that his secret to success was to write jokes every single day. To ensure that he did so, he kept a big calendar and marked each day with a big red X when he completed writing.[27]

Seinfeld explained, "After a few days you'll have a chain. Just keep at it and the chain will grow longer every day. You'll like seeing that chain, especially when you get a few weeks under your belt. Your only job is to not break the chain."

This technique has proven successful for any behavior you make routine or habit you might want to break. Simply set your goal and mark each day you achieve that goal. As the chain gets longer, you'll feel motivated to complete the task at hand so as not to break the chain.

I integrated this concept into my task management app, priorigami. Each day you select and complete your top three priority tasks, you are congratulated. The app tracks the number of tasks you complete each day showing you how many days you've gone without "breaking the chain." It feels good to see when you're hitting your goal each day.

DAILY TASKS COMPLETED

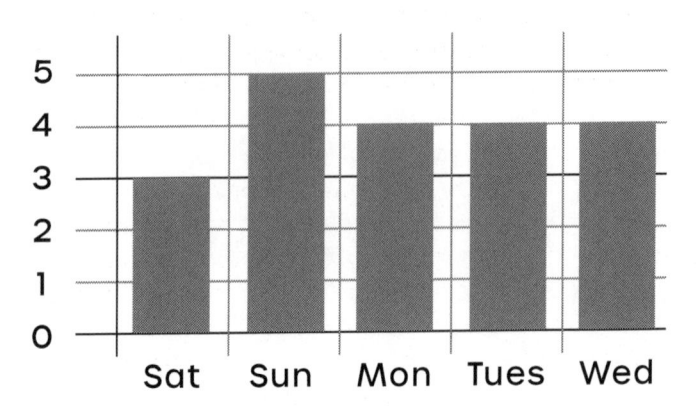

	Sat	Sun	Mon	Tues	Wed
	3	5	4	4	4

There are days when you'll be less productive and unable to complete your top three tasks. On these days, you "break the chain" falling short of your goal.

DAILY TASKS COMPLETED

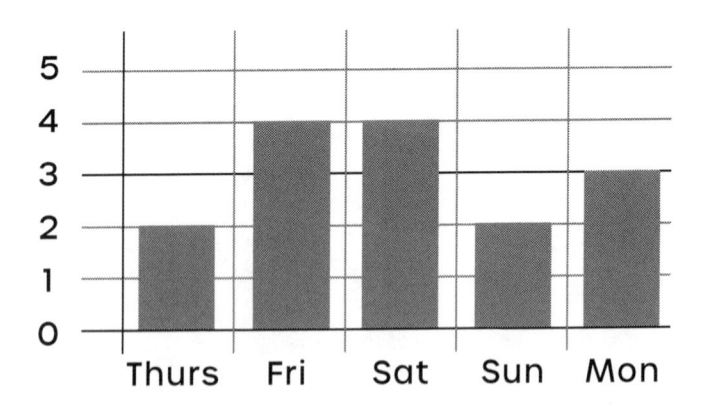

	Thurs	Fri	Sat	Sun	Mon
	2	4	4	2	3

The reason this technique works is that it asks you to break down lofty goals into tangible daily tasks. Instead of fixating on becoming a better writer, the focus is on making time to write each day. Or, instead of obsessing on losing fifteen pounds, the focus shifts to making time to exercise daily.

Once you get started, you will notice that each day, the task that will get you to your goal gets easier as it becomes part of your routine. The visual of the chain on a calendar or chart reinforces the behavior. The longer the chain grows, the more motivated you become. How long is your Wordle streak, for example?

When I was relaunching priorigami, I lost access to my to-do list for a few weeks and had to work primarily out of my phone's Notes app. I noticed that I wasn't as productive in completing my tasks. Without the daily reminder to pick my top three priorities for the day and the reinforcement of the "chain," I wasn't as focused or motivated.

TRY THIS

Identify something you want to achieve or change. Set a daily goal that can be achieved, measured, and tracked. Get a calendar and a marker and place it somewhere you will see daily. Mark each day you complete your goal. How does it feel? How many days can you go before breaking the chain?

READ MORE

Make SMARTer Resolutions
Bringing Your Vision to Life
Creating New Habits

CREATING NEW HABITS

By now you're probably thinking that while all of this sounds good, it's a lot of work. Constant mental gymnastics just to keep up with everything seems quite overwhelming. Wouldn't it just be easier to wing it and hope for the best?

To make productivity work for you, introduce one or two new techniques at a time and practice them until they become habitual. Once a new habit is created it becomes rote within a month or so and you won't need to think about it anymore. At that point, you can tackle another one or two new methods. If you try to do it all at once, it will be overwhelming.

So, how are new habits created? In his book, *The Power of Habit: Why We Do What We Do in Life and Business*, Charles Duhigg breaks down the science of habit formation. He explains that the habit loop consists of these three elements: a cue, a routine, and a reward. The key to successfully creating new habits is to develop a routine that is triggered every time a "cue" arises and to follow up with a reward to reinforce the routine.[28] You can also apply this loop to break bad habits as well.

For example, say you want to start drinking more water. Whenever you start to feel thirsty, set a new routine to grab water and not soda or any other drink. To create a new process or system for yourself, consider buying a new water bottle to keep with you and make it more convenient to grab over something else.

Also, think about the triggers that make you crave coffee or soda and consider ways you could fill that need with water instead. Would it help to add some flavoring drops to your water? As your intake of water increases don't forget to reward yourself. Maybe treat yourself to a soda on a Friday after you've achieved your water goals during that week.

When I was pregnant with my son, I stopped drinking coffee and sodas. When he was born, I decided not to start back up again. Over the years, I developed a habit to drink water whenever I got thirsty and now I don't even miss caffeinated drinks. The biggest benefit of creating a new habit is that, at some point in the near future, you won't even remember what you're missing because it will have been replaced by a new routine.

So, how long does it take to create a new habit? There's a lot of research and debate on how long the process takes. Back in the 1960s in his book, *Psycho-Cybernetics, A New Way to Get More Living Out of Life*, Dr. Maxwell Martz started a popular myth that it took 21 days to create a new habit.[29] Unfortunately, the answer isn't so straightforward and honestly, the timeline can vary greatly depending on the habit you are trying to create.

Instead of focusing on the timeline, concentrate on the process and keep your eye on the desired result. James Clear summarized his book, *Atomic Habits: An Easy and Proven Way to Build Good Habits and Break Bad Ones*, by saying, "If you're having trouble changing your habits, the problem isn't you. The problem is your system."[30]

TRY THIS

What new habit would you like to create, or which bad habit would you like to break? What are some cues that can trigger this behavior?

Develop a new process or system for you to respond to those triggers. Don't forget to reward yourself as you make progress.

READ MORE

Bringing Your Vision to Life
Productivity Requires Perseverance
Don't Break the Chain

THE PRODUCTIVITY WORKOUT

Are you trying to lose weight, eat healthier, exercise regularly? Many of us have goals around living a healthier lifestyle, but it's hard because it takes planning, discipline, and time. Becoming more productive isn't any different.

I often hear people say that they want to get more done. They would like to be more organized and efficient, but they won't do anything differently to get there. It's almost as if they hope these things will magically appear like an Amazon order placed only hours earlier. If only.

Living a healthy lifestyle requires exercising three to five times a week, walking 10,000 steps a day, and a healthy diet of 2,000 calories, give or take. None of this happens without proactive planning and a dedicated daily routine. Similarly, to increase your productivity and efficiency, you need to develop and follow your own productivity workout.

SET SMART GOALS

To get started, you first need to clearly define your goals. It's not enough to say you want to be more organized or productive. You need to be able to openly articulate goals that can be easily tracked and measured. As Yogi Berra famously said:

> "If you don't know where you're going, you might not get there."

TOOLS

To improve your fitness, you may need an exercise coach, workout equipment, healthy recipes, a fitness tracker app, and other tools to help you achieve your goals. Without these tools, achieving your goal will be more challenging.

Similarly, you will need certain tools to help you become more productive. First, use a calendar to schedule your time, including work meetings, appointments, and reminders and to block off personal time. Also, make sure you maintain a single to-do list to track your tasks. Finally, obtain a journal to keep your notes in one place for easy reference when needed.

DISCIPLINE

Now, you need a plan to put your workout in action. Begin by scheduling an hour each week in your calendar for planning. During this time, review and confirm your appointments and meetings for the week ahead. Identify big items that need to be done and schedule them into your calendar to ensure they get done. For critically important items, schedule it twice. Be sure to update your to-do list.

Each day, either the night before or at the start of the new day, review your list and select your top three priorities for the day. It's fine for your priorities to change throughout the day and can be adjusted as needed. Also, don't forget to delete or delay or delegate unimportant tasks.

TRY THIS

Find an hour this week and block it off to develop your own productivity workout. First, identify your goals and determine what tools you will need to get you there. Schedule time each week for planning and for setting your daily priorities.

READ MORE

Achieve Balance By Maximizing Your Tools
Make SMARTer Resolutions
Productivity Requires Perseverance

JUST SAY NO!

Almost all productivity experts agree that one crucial way to improve your productivity and focus is to learn how to say no. For me, this has been a continual struggle. In fact, I probably need to re-read this chapter once a week as a reminder.

I am a people-pleaser, and I enjoy helping others. I like to be asked to do things, and I thrive on getting things done. I always volunteered to be the notetaker in meetings and would offer to plan company events. I would stop what I was working on whenever someone needed a moment of my time and soon earned the title of "go-to person" whenever anything needed to get done.

I was so busy doing tasks for other people that my most important tasks either weren't getting done or were falling to the bottom of my list. To compensate, I would stay at work longer or go to bed later to take care of the things that I needed to get done.

Finding myself in this situation too many times made me realize I would have to start saying no. To help me get comfortable with this approach, I followed the mantra:

*Just because you **can** do it, doesn't mean you **should** do it.*

I thoughtfully considered how to start confidently declining some tasks. Now, before blindly taking on something new, I ask myself to decide which tasks I should take on and which I should pass on.

IS IT JUST BUSY WORK?

When asked to help with a task, I assess how it will benefit me. If I find that I won't gain knowledge or value from doing it, it's easier for me to turn it down, and I will feel better knowing I did so.

CAN SOMEONE ELSE DO IT?

If someone else can easily handle the requested task or may even benefit from the challenge of taking it on, it's easier for me to decline and suggest delegating that task. Often, if someone can learn or gain a new skill or experience from doing a task, they will probably be happy to do it.

DOES IT EVEN NEED TO BE DONE?

Many times, we do things just to do them. I find that if you think critically about how important a task is, you may find that it doesn't need to be done. Is this a "must have" or a "nice to have?" What would happen if the task didn't get done? Try to work only on the things that matter most.

TRY THIS

Look over your to-do list. Are there tasks on your list that you shouldn't be doing? How can you comfortably say no? Try pushing back on the tasks that prevent you from focusing on completing your most important tasks.

READ MORE

The Fallacy of Doing It All
The Prioritization Puzzle
The Three R's of Productivity

ASKING FOR HELP IS NOT A WEAKNESS

This is another chapter I should re-read daily. No matter how much I preach, I still have a hard time putting this concept into practice. Deep down, I know I am not meant to do everything myself, however I somehow have it ingrained in me that asking for help is a sign of weakness. To me, it's an admission that I'm not good enough or equipped to get something done myself. Also, I really don't like the idea of inconveniencing someone else with a task I can do myself.

The worst habit I've developed is expecting others to know when I need help before I have to ask. When I get home from the grocery store with a car full of bags, I hope my family will stop what they are doing to help me. When they don't jump up, I feel resentment, often making my discontentment known by making the most noise possible.

This petty behavior is as ineffective as it sounds!

I have to remind myself I didn't raise a family of mind-readers. It's much simpler for everyone, and far less passive-aggressive, if I ask for what I want. When I do, I find that they are happy to help out, and in the case of grocery day, everything gets put away much faster and with far less banging around.

Here are three reasons why asking for help is actually a strength, not a weakness.

PEOPLE WANT TO BE WANTED

For the most part, people like to help. It makes them feel needed. I'm genuinely honored when others ask for my help. So, when I can use an extra hand, I remind myself that most would be glad to pitch in to support me.

CONTRIBUTING MAKES PEOPLE FEEL VALUED

When someone asks you to help them, it's because you have something you can offer to them. I remind myself of the studies that show that kids who help with chores around the house are happier and more successful in life because helping makes them feel more capable, accountable, and independent. These kids are also more responsible, have higher self-esteem and better time management skills.

TEAMWORK YIELDS BETTER RESULTS

When people come together to tackle something, the output is always better. For example, if you ask someone to review your work, the final product will likely be better than if it had only one set of eyes on it. Also, cleaning the house with a family member or accomplishing a DIY project with a friend is more fun than tackling it by yourself.

TRY THIS

What could you use help with? What's holding you back from asking for help? How would the person feel if you asked for their assistance? Could it end up being a win-win situation where asking for their help would not only help you, but would benefit them as well?

READ MORE

The Fallacy of Doing It All
The Prioritization Puzzle
The Three R's of Productivity

FEEDBACK IS A GIFT

Whenever I get lost, stuck, or confused, I look outwardly to receive input from those around me. There's nothing more valuable than honest, candid feedback to achieve clarity and get back on track. Unfortunately, during challenging times, our tendency is to look inward in an attempt to figure it out on our own or wait until it resolves itself.

I'll be the first to admit that I don't have all the answers. I can't solve every problem alone and I certainly don't always have the best ideas. The way I have gotten through challenging times in my life is through asking for feedback, collaborating with others, and sharing ideas. Every great idea results from the sum of smaller notions.

It's easy to give and receive positive feedback, a great motivator in itself, but not always the most helpful. By far, the most productive feedback is constructive, which aims to improve the outcome or lead to a more innovative solution. The fastest way to get to a great result is to ask others who have been in a similar situation to share what worked, what didn't work, or what you may be missing.

How you present your feedback will determine how it is received. There's no need to be mean or condescending when offering alternative suggestions as potential thoughts or ideas. Here are some ways to start your feedback conversation:

- Have you considered...?
- What if you...?
- How about...?
- I wonder if this might work...?
- This is interesting, how did you come up with...?

If you are the one receiving the feedback, keep an open mind and listen. No need to get defensive even if they are calling your baby ugly. Seek to understand their ideas and perspectives.

Often, I let feedback sink in for a day or two before responding. There's no reason to react immediately when you may be feeling hurt. The best response is to thank them for their feedback and take time to thoroughly consider their input.

So, now it's my turn. I've been writing this book in my head for many years. Please email me at monishalongacre@productivity101.biz and let me know your thoughts about the book, what you've learned, or anything else that comes to mind. The gift of your feedback will help me understand your challenges so we can better support each other.

Please share your feedback by leaving a review on Goodreads, Amazon, or another review site of your choice.

Thank you!

> **TRY THIS**
>
> Stuck on solving a problem? Gather a few people with different experiences or perspectives and hold a brainstorming session. You'll be amazed at the number of ideas you can gather in less than an hour.

> **READ MORE**
>
> The Importance of Why
> Asking for Help is Not a Weakness

UNTIL NEXT TIME...

Thank you for joining me on this journey. I hope you found some tips and tricks that you've been able to incorporate into your routine or put into practice. Hopefully the time you've invested in reading this book will free up even more of your time in the future.

I hope you'll keep this book nearby and pull it out when you find yourself stuck or struggling to keep up with it all. Think of it as your "personal productivity genie" ready to jump in and help out whenever needed.

Better yet, give a copy of this book to a friend or colleague who might benefit from some of the ideas. There's nothing better than finding a good resource and passing it forward with the hope it will also help others.

The good, or perhaps the bad news, is that this journey never ends. So until we're back together again, go forth and do amazing things using *Practical Productivity*!

And, one final task. If you can write a review of this book for me, I'd be eternally grateful.

APPENDIX

1 Newport, Cal. *Deep Work: Rules For Focused Success in a Distracted World.* United States: Loudly, 2024.

2 Bailey, Chris. *Hyperfocus: How to Be More Productive in a Distracted World.* New York: Penguin Books, 2019.

3 Branson, Richard. "My (Usual) Daily Routine: Virgin." Virgin.com, April 6, 2017. https://www.virgin.com/branson-family/richard-branson-blog/my-usual-daily-routine.

4 Pink, Daniel. "Pinkcast 1.2: A Simple Trick for Getting the Right Stuff Done: Daniel H. Pink." Daniel H. Pink | The official site of author Daniel Pink, July 25, 2019. https://www.danpink.com/pinkcast/pinkcast-1-2-a-simple-trick-for-getting-the-right-stuff-done/.

5 Hauser, Fran. *Embrace the Work, Love Your Career: A Guided Workbook for Realizing Your Career Goals with Clarity, Intention, and Confidence.* Oakland, CA: The Collective Book Studio, 2022.

6 McKeown, Greg. *Essentialism: The Disciplined Pursuit of Less.* London: Virgin Books, 2021.

7 Greenfield, Robin. "All My 111 Possessions…" Robin Greenfield, March 21, 2016. https://www.robingreenfield.org/possessions/.

8 Greenfield, Robin. "My 44 Possessions: Everything I Own Fits in My Backpack." Robin Greenfield, February 28, 2020. https://www.robingreenfield.org/44possessions/.

9 Mangan, Lucy. "When the French Clock off at 6pm, They Really Mean It." *The Guardian*, April 9, 2014. https://www.theguardian.com/money/shortcuts/2014/apr/09/french-6pm-labour-agreement-work-emails-out-of-office.

10 Alderman, Liz. "In Sweden, an Experiment Turns Shorter Workdays into Bigger Gains." *The New York Times*, May 20, 2016. https://www.nytimes.com/2016/05/21/business/international/in-sweden-an-experiment-turns-shorter-workdays-into-bigger-gains.html.

11 "The Results Are in: The UK's Four-Day Week Pilot." The Autonomy Institute, February 2023. https://autonomy.work/portfolio/uk4dwpilotresults/.

12 Laborde, Susan. "Mobile App Download Statistics Everyone Should Know in 2023." Techreport, May 28, 2024. https://techreport.com/statistics/software-web/mobile-app-download-statistics/.

13 Dutton, Judy. "Make Your Bed, Change Your Life?" *Psychology Today*, August 16, 2012. https://www.psychologytoday.com/intl/blog/brain-candy/201208/make-your-bed-change-your-life.

14 McRaven, William. "Adm. Mcraven Urges Graduates to Find Courage to Change the World." *UT News*, May 16, 2014. https://news.utexas.edu/2014/05/16/mcraven-urges-graduates-to-find-courage-to-change-the-world/.

15 Tracy, Brian.. *Eat That Frog!: 21 Great Ways to Stop Procrastinating and Get More Done In Less Time*. S.l.: BERRETT-KOEHLER, 2025.

16 Kounios, John, and Beeman, Mark. *The Eureka Factor: Aha Moments, Creative Insight, and the Brain*. London: Windmill Books, 2016.

17 Allen, David. *Getting Things Done: The Art of Stress-Free Productivity*. Must Read Summaries, 2012.

18 "Meeting Statistics You Should Know for 2024." Pumble Learn, November 12, 2024. https://pumble.com/learn/communication/meeting-statistics.

19 Whiting, Geoff. "Work-Life Balance Statistics for 2024: A Global Perspective." Hubstaff Blog, August 13, 2024. https://hubstaff.com/blog/work-life-balance-statistics/.

20 Diamond, Dan. "Just 8% of People Achieve Their New Year's Resolutions. Here's How They Do It." *Forbes*, January 2, 2013. https://www.forbes.com/sites/dandiamond/2013/01/01/just-8-of-people-achieve-their-new-years-resolutions-heres-how-they-did-it/.

21 Covey, Stephen R., Covey, Sean and Collins, James C.. *The 7 Habits of Highly Effective People: Powerful Lessons in Personal Change*. Ashland, OR: Blackstone Publishing, 2023.

22 "7 Big Rocks - The Productivity System." YouTube, December 27, 2013. https://www.youtube.com/watch?v=fmV0gXpXwDU

23 Borsheim, Sherry. "Organizing & Time Management Statistics." Simply Productive, April 23, 2014. https://www.simplyproductive.com/2012/03/time-management-statistics/.

24 Duckworth, Angela. Grit: *The Power of Passion and Perseverance.* New York, NY: Scribner, 2018.

25 Duhigg, Charles, and Chamberlain, Mike. *Smarter Faster Better: The Secrets of Being Productive in Life and Business.* Westminster, MD, New York: Books on Tape ; Penguin House Audio, 2016.

26 Onque, Renée. "Americans Check Their Phones 144 Times a Day: How You Can Break Bad Digital Habits." CNBC, April 17, 2024. https://www.cnbc.com/2024/04/17/digital-wellbeing-expert-tips-for-being-mindful-of-your-phone-use.html.

27 Trapani, Gina. "'Don't Break the Chain' to Build a New Habit." Lifehacker, November 3, 2023. https://lifehacker.com/jerry-seinfelds-productivity-secret-281626.

28 Duhigg, Charles. *The Power of Habit: Why We Do What We Do in Life and Business.* summary. Kennett Square, Pa, Norwood, Mass.: Soundview Executive Book Summaries ; Distributed by Books24x7.com, 2012.

29 Maltz, Maxwell. *Psycho-Cybernetics: A New Way to Get More Living Out of Life.* Waco, Tx: Success Motivation Institute, 1966.

30 Clear, James. *Atomic Habits: An Easy & Proven Way to Build Good Habits & Break Bad Ones.* Navaar LLC, 2020.

PRIORIGAMI
THE ART OF PRODUCTIVITY

This is not just another to-do list app. priorigami will help you manage, prioritize, and complete tasks more efficiently so you can spend more time doing the things that really matter in life.

Getting things done doesn't have to be overwhelming.

It can be simple and fun, too!

| Enter Tasks | Prioritize | Track Your Progress |

Don't feel overwhelmed by your list of tasks or deflated by having too much to do.

Download priorigami and immediately enjoy the benefits of increased productivity.

www.priorigami.com

REFERENCES

Throughout this book, I have cited a variety of books, podcasts, and other resources that have helped me on my own productivity journey which are listed below. I have also included books I didn't mention directly but might be helpful to you on your journey especially if you want to dig in deeper into specific topics or concepts.

BOOKS

Atomic Habits, James Clear

Death by Meeting, Patrick Lencioni

Deep Work: Rules for Focused Success in a Distracted World, Cal Newport

Drive: The Surprising Truth About What Motivates Us, Daniel Pink

Eat That Frog!: 21 Great Ways to Stop Procrastinating and Get More Done in Less Time, Brian Tracy

Embrace the Work, Love Your Career, Fran Hauser

Essentialism: The Disciplined Pursuit of Less, Greg McKeown

Essential Zen Habits, Leo Babauta

Getting Things Done: The Art of Stress-Free Productivity, David Allen

Grit: The Power of Passion and Perseverance, Angela Duckworth

Hooked: How to Build Habit-Forming Products, Nir Eyal

How to Calm Your Mind, Chris Bailey

Hyperfocus: How to Manage Your Attention in a World of Distraction, Chris Bailey

Indistractable: How to Control Your Attention and Choose Your Life, Nir Eyal

Listful Living, Paula Rizzo

Make Your Bed: Small things that can change your life ... and maybe the world, William H. McRaven

Psycho-Cybernetics, A New Way to Get More Living Out of Life, Dr. Maxwell Martz

Quiet: The Power of Introverts in a World That Can't Stop Talking, Susan Cain

Smarter, Better, Faster, Charles Duhigg

Start with Why: How Great Leaders Inspire Everyone to Take Action, Simon Sinek

The Eureka Factor: Aha Moments, Creative Insight, and the Brain, John Kounios

The Five Dysfunctions of a Team, Patrick Lencioni

The 4-Hour Workweek: Escape 9-5, Live Anywhere, and Join the New Rich, Timothy Ferriss

The Productivity Project, Chris Bailey

The One Thing: The Surprisingly Simple Truth Behind Extraordinary Results, Gary Keller and Jay Papsan

The Outstanding Organization: Generate Business Results by Eliminating Chaos and Building the Foundation for Everyday Excellence, Karen Martin

The Power of Habit: Why We Do What We Do in Life and Business, Charles Duhigg

The 7 Habits Of Highly Effective People, Stephen R Covey

BLOGS

Richard Branson's Blog
www.virgin.com/branson-family/richard-branson-blog

Inspiration and Education from the Mind of Robin Greenfield
www.robingreenfield.org/blog/

The Pinkcast by Daniel Pink
www.danpink.com/pinkcast/

Seinfeld: The Blog About Nothing
www.seinfeldfanatic.wordpress.com/

RESOURCES

AnyList - www.anylist.com
One app for stress-free shopping, cooking, and meal planning.

Canva - www.canva.com/create/vision-boards
Craft a stunning virtual vision board for every area of your life that will inspire and motivate you.

Goodreads - www.goodreads.com
Keep track of all your books – the ones you've read and the ones you want to read and get recommendations too.

KanbanFlow - www.kanbanflow.com
Create a visual overview of your team projects to easily track progress, assign tasks, and set deadlines.

Listography - www.lisanola.com/journals
Guided journals are the ultimate tool for creating a unique autobiography entirely in list form

priorigami: the art of productivity - www.priorigami.com
Not just another to-do list app, priorigami will help you manage, prioritize, and complete tasks more efficiently.

Smartduvet - www.smartduvet.com
A self-making duvet that makes your bed so you don't have to.

ACKNOWLEDGMENTS

Sometimes a casual meeting alters the trajectory of your journey many years later. It's not planned or expected or even realized for quite some time. Feeding off the excitement of launching my task management app, I was introduced to Jeff Hilimire, a self-professed productivity aficionado. Little did I know at the time that he would go on to found a publishing company, and I would go on to write and publish this book. I am eternally grateful to Jeff and the entire team at Ripples Media for encouraging and helping me bring this book to life.

Every job I have ever taken, I have taken on as a learning opportunity. I am deeply appreciative of the many managers, leaders, mentors, and colleagues who challenged me professionally beginning with my first job at Lotus Development Corp to serving as the webmaster at EY to managing weather.com at The Weather Channel. Each role pushed me to develop these strategies and formulate this framework. These opportunities also gave me the confidence to seek elevated roles in various tech startups and even start a business, develop an app, and write this book.

While my quest to optimize my time and energy was innate, I must acknowledge the productivity experts who have come before me and paved the way to establish this topic as a well researched field of study. Many of my recommendations have stemmed from some of their thoughts, experiments, and experiences. I am especially thankful for Chris and Paula who willingly stepped up to support me and this book.

This book would not have been finished without my "early adopters" who enthusiastically took on the challenge of reading advanced copies of it, providing honest feedback, and shaping it into this final product. Thank you Andrew, Heather, Nicole, Laura, Vandana, Lisa, and Ayesha.

Honestly, this book wouldn't exist without my immediate family. I am forever indebted to my parents, Verinder and Manjula, who raised me with high expectations coupled with a belief that I could do anything that I set my mind to doing. And, if it hadn't been for my husband's demanding career along with my children's dedication to two sports each, and our family's desire to participate in countless activities and experiences, I wouldn't have needed to figure out the best ways to keep up with it all. So, my immense gratitude goes to Keith, Maya, and Jayson for challenging me every single day to develop this framework to keep all the balls in the air, ensure all the pieces came together, and do everything possible to win the game of life!

ABOUT THE AUTHOR

Monisha Longacre is a seasoned operations executive, entrepreneur, and author of *Practical Productivity: A Guide to Surviving Life's Juggling Act*. With over three decades of experience scaling and optimizing technology businesses, she brings a uniquely practical approach to both organizational and personal effectiveness. As COO of multiple SaaS companies she has consistently driven innovation and growth while maintaining operational excellence.

Throughout her career, Monisha has bridged the worlds of technology and consumer experience at industry leaders including The Weather Channel, McKesson, EY, and Lotus Development. Her entrepreneurial spirit has led her to found several successful EdTech and HRTech startups, including Productivity 101, where she provides expertise and tools to help professionals maximize their effectiveness. She is also the creator of priorigami: the art of productivity, a task management mobile app that embodies her practical approach to getting things done.

A graduate of the University of Virginia with a bachelor's degree in Communications and Boston University with a master's in Corporate Public Relations, Monisha combines deep technical knowledge with exceptional communication skills. She is actively involved in women's leadership development, serving in key positions across multiple networking organizations.

Based in Atlanta, Georgia, where she lives with her husband (and occasionally returning adult children), Monisha constantly seeks new experiences to add to her bucket list. When not optimizing productivity or mentoring the next generation of women leaders, she can be found traveling, reading, or testing new productivity strategies in her own life.

Made in the USA
Columbia, SC
20 May 2025